MARRIAGE:
THE ROCK ON WHICH THE FAMILY IS BUILT

William E. May

MARRIAGE: The Rock on Which the Family Is Built

Second edition

IGNATIUS PRESS   SAN FRANCISCO

Original edition:
© 1995 by Ignatius Press, San Francisco

Cover photographs by istockphoto.com
Cover design by Riz Boncan Marsella

To the Memory of Pope John Paul II
Champion of Marriage and the Family

CONTENTS

INTRODUCTION TO THE
SECOND EDITION

Two of the more tragic consequences of the attacks on families, which should be rooted in the life-long marriage of one man and one woman, are the alarming increase in the number of children who grow up in single parent, typically fatherless, families, and the impact this has had on our nation's culture. Nonetheless, the attacks continue, as I shall now show.

Evidence of Attacks on and Defenses of Marriage and Family

I began the "Introduction" to the First Chapter of the first edition with data showing the risks facing families, and in particular children, in the 1990s, citing material from a report entitled *Beyond Rhetoric: A New American Agenda for Children and Families*, issued in the summer of 1991 by a National Commission on Children established in 1987 by the Congress and President of the United States. Now, more than a decade later, attacks on marriage and the family have intensified throughout the world, as many studies clearly demonstrate. For example, the investigators who prepared *The Revolution in Parenthood: The Emerging Global Clash between Adult Rights and Children's Needs* describe the scope of these attacks as follows:

> Around the world, the two-person, mother-father model of parenthood is being fundamentally challenged. In Canada . . . the controversial law that brought about same-sex marriage quietly included the provision to erase the term "natural parent" across the board in federal law, replacing it with the term "legal parent". . . . In Spain, after the recent legalization of same-sex marriage the legislature changed the birth certificates for all children in that nation to read "Progenitor A" and "Progenitor B" instead of "mother" and "father."

With that change, the words "mother" and "father" were struck from the first document issued to every newborn by the state. . . . In the United States, courts often must determine who the legal parents are among the many adults who might be involved in planning, conceiving, birthing, and raising a child. In a growing practice, judges in several states have seized upon the idea of "psychological" parenthood to award legal parent status to adults who are not related to children by blood, adoption, or marriage. . . . Successes in the same-sex marriage debate have encouraged group marriage advocates who wish to break open the two-person under-standing of marriage and parenthood. . . . Nearly all of these steps, and many more, are being taken in the name of adult rights to form families they choose. But what about the children?[1]

In its conclusion the report notes:

When society changes marriage it changes parenthood . . . the two-natural-parent, mother-father model is falling away, replaced with the idea that children are fine with any one or more adults being called their parents, so long as the appointed parents are nice peo-ple. . . . Those of us who are concerned can and should take up and lead a debate about the lives of children and the future of parenthood. As we launch this conversation, a guiding principle could be this: When there is a clash between adult rights and children's needs, the interests of the more vulnerable party—in this case, the children—should take precedence. A great deal of evidence supports the idea that children, on average, do best when raised by their own mothers and fathers.[2]

Similarly, Elizabeth Marquardt, author of *Between Two Worlds: The Inner Lives of Children of Divorce*, summarizes her findings in this way:

The inner conflict handed to children of divorce has conse-quences. Among the nationally representative findings [are these]:

---

[1] *The Revolution in Parenthood: The Emerging Global Clash between Adult Rights and Children's Needs* (New York: Institute for American Values, 2006), pp. 5–6. The principal investigator was Elizabeth Marquardt; among other members of the committee were David Blankenhorn, Maggie Galagher, Robert George, and Dan Browning.

[2] Ibid., pp. 32–33.

Young adults from divorced families are much more likely to say that, growing up, they felt like a different person with each of their parents. They are much more likely to say their divorced parents were polar opposites, even in the majority of cases when their parents did not conflict a lot. They are much more likely to say that they kept secrets for their parents, even when their parents did not ask them to. They are more likely to say they feared resembling one of their parents too much, because it might alienate them from the other parent. They are much more likely to say they often felt alone as a child. They are more likely to say that at times they felt like an outsider in their home. The moral confusion and isolation these children experience impact their spiritual journeys as well. Very little research has been done on the religious and spiritual experience of children of divorce. New findings reported in this book show that, as a group, when they grow up, children of divorce are less religious than their peers from intact families. But some become much more religious as a result of their parents' divorce (with more of them agreeing, for instance, that God became the father or parent they never had in real life) while some become less. Children of divorce are more likely to agree that the suffering they witness in the world and in their own lives makes them doubt the existence of a loving God. They are more likely to feel that no one really understands them and more of them feel that the hardships in their life come from God.[3]

The plague of single-parent families and the terrible problems that such families experience are as debilitating now as they were when the first edition of this book was published, as data provided by the Parents without Partners organization illustrate:

As of 2000 an estimated 13.5 million single parents had custody of 21.7 million children under 21 years of age whose other parent lived somewhere else. The proportion of the population made up by married couples with children decreased from 40% in 1970 to 24% in 2000. One-parent families numbered over 12 million in 2000. Single-parent households increased from 9% in 1990 to 16% of all households by 2000. Of all custodial parents, 85% were mothers

[3] Elizabeth Marquardt, *Between Two Worlds: The Inner Lives of Children of Divorce* (New York: Crown Books, 2006), pp. x–xi. This summary of the book is given by Marquardt at http://betweentwoworlds.org/comments/?cat=4.

and 15% were fathers. Births among unmarried women increased and the proportion of never-married parents increased. Single-mother families increased from 7 million in 1999 to 10 million in 2000. Today 13.8 million children (23%) under 15 live with single mothers, 2.7 million (5%) live with single fathers. The proportion of single-mother families grew to 26% and single-father families grew to 5% by 2000 (from 12% and 1% respectively in 1970). Forty-six per cent of single-mother households contain more than one child. Overall, about 26.2% of all children under 21 living in families have a parent not living at home.[4]

On the other hand, evidence gathered by social scientists demonstrates that marriage between one man and one woman is good for them, their children, and society. For example, in 2005 a team of social scientists headed by W. Bradford Wilcox issued *Why Marriage Matters, Second Edition: Twenty-Six Conclusions from the Social Sciences*.[5] As the subtitle indicates, in their study they list twenty-six conclusions, divided into four major areas:

Family

1. Marriage increases the likelihood that fathers and mothers have good relationships with their children.
2. Cohabitation is not the functional equivalent of marriage.
3. Growing up outside an intact family increases the likelihood that children will themselves divorce or become unwed parents.
4. Marriage is virtually a universal phenomenon.
5. Marriage, and a normative commitment to marriage, foster high-quality relationships between adults, as well as between parents and children.
6. Marriage has important biosocial consequences for adults and children.

[4] See http://www.parentswithoutpartners.org/Support1.htm.

[5] New York: Institute for American Values. The study was done under the chairmanship of W. Bradford Wilcox of the University of Virginia, William Doherty of the University of Minnesota, Norval Glenn of the University of Texas, and Linda Waite of the University of Chicago. Twelve other social scientists formed the team that produced the study.

Economics

7. Divorce and unmarried childbearing increase poverty rates for both children and mothers.
8. Married couples seem to build more wealth on average than singles or cohabiting couples.
9. Marriage reduces poverty and material hardship for disadvantaged women and their children.
10. Minorities benefit economically from marriage.
11. Married men earn more money than do single men with similar education and job histories.
12. Parental divorce (or failure to marry) appears to increase children's risk of school failure.
13. Parental divorce reduces the likelihood that children will graduate from college and achieve high-status jobs.

Physical Health and Longevity

14. Children who live with their own two married parents enjoy better physical health on average than do children in other family forms.
15. Parental marriage is associated with a sharply lower risk of infant mortality.
16. Marriage is associated with reduced rates of alcohol and substance abuse for both adults and teens.
17. Married people, especially married men, have longer life expectancies than do otherwise similar singles.
18. Marriage is associated with better health and lower rates of injury, illness, and disability for both men and women.
19. Marriage seems to be associated with better health among minorities and the poor.

Mental Health and Emotional Well-being

20. Children whose parents divorce have higher rates of psychological distress and mental illness.
21. Divorce appears to increase significantly the risk of suicide.

22. Married mothers have lower rates of depression than do single or cohabiting mothers.
23. Boys raised in single-parent families are more likely to engage in delinquent and criminal behavior.
24. Marriage appears to reduce the risk that adults will be either perpetrators or victims of crime.
25. Married women appear to have a lower risk of experiencing domestic violence than do cohabiting or dating women.
26. A child who is not living with his own two married parents is at a greater risk for suffering child abuse.[6]

Even more remarkably, social science studies show that failure to follow the truths of Pope Paul VI's affirmation in *Humanae vitae* would cause serious debilitating harm to families, women, and children. W. Bradford Wilcox has demonstrated this in several masterful articles.[7] Wilcox shows that the findings of such social scientists as Robert Michael and George Akerlof definitely support Pope Paul's affirmation. Wilcox focuses on two important essays by Akerlof in which this leading sociologist details findings that vindicate Paul VI's prophetic warnings about the social consequences of contraception for morality and men.

Wilcox points out that Akerlof, in an article published in the *Quarterly Journal of Economics* asked why there was such a dramatic increase in illegitimacy in the United States from 1965 to 1990—from 24 percent to 64 percent among African-Americans, and from 3 percent to 18 percent among whites, even though "public health advocates had predicted that the widespread availability of

[6] Ibid., pp. 10–11. On pages 12–32 the authors of the study provide detailed empirical data to support these twenty-six conclusions.

[7] See the following: W. Bradford Wilcox, "Social Science and the Vindication of Catholic Moral Teaching", in *The Church, Marriage, and the Family: Proceedings from the 27th Annual Convention of the Fellowship of Catholic Scholars, September 24–26, 2004, Pittsburgh, PA*, ed. Kenneth Whitehead (South Bend: St. Augustine's Press, 2007), pp. 330–40. Unfortunately, this very fine paper, given in September 2004, had to wait until May 2007 to be published. Wilcox, however, summarized the principal findings he reported in that paper and updated them in his essay, "The Facts of Life and Marriage: Social Science and the Vindication of Christian Moral Teaching", *Touchstone* (February 2005), and I will use this source here.

contraception and abortion would reduce illegitimacy, not increase it."

> So what happened? ... [After noting] that "technological innovation creates both winners and losers," Akerlof showed that "in this case the introduction of widespread effective contraception ... put traditional women with an interest in marriage and children at a 'competitive disadvantage' in the relationship 'market' compared to modern women who took a more hedonistic approach to sex and relationships. The contraceptive revolution also reduced the costs of sex for women and men, insofar as the threat of childbearing was taken off the table, especially as abortion became widely available in the 1970s."

As a result of this, Wilcox continues, Akerlof pointed out that "the norm of premarital sexual abstinence all but vanished in the wake of the technology shock." Women felt free or obligated to have sex before marriage. For instance, Akerlof found that the percentage of girls sixteen and under reporting sexual activity surged in 1970 and 1971 as contraception and abortion became common in many states throughout the country.

> Thus, the sexual revolution left traditional or moderate women who wanted to avoid premarital sex or contraception "immiserated" because they could not compete with women who had no serious objection to premarital sex, and they could no longer elicit a promise of marriage from boyfriends in the event [that] they got pregnant. Boyfriends, of course, could say that pregnancy was their girlfriends' choice. So men were less likely to agree to a shotgun marriage in the event of a pregnancy....

> Thus, many traditional women ended up having sex and having children out of wedlock, while many of the permissive women ended up having sex and contracepting or aborting so as to avoid childbearing. This explains in large part why the contraceptive revolution was associated with an increase in both abortion and illegitimacy.

In his second article, published in *The Economic Journal* in 1998, Akerlof argues that another key outworking of the contraceptive revolution was the disappearance of marriage—shotgun and otherwise—for men. Contraception and abortion allowed men to put off marriage, even in cases where they had fathered a child. Consequently, the fraction of young men who were married in the United States dropped precipitously. Between 1968 and 1993 the percentage of men from 25 to 34 who were married with children fell from 66 percent to 40 percent. Accordingly, young men did not benefit from the domesticating influence of wives and children.

Instead, they could continue to hang out with their young male friends, and were thus more vulnerable to the drinking, partying, tomcatting, and worse that is associated with unsupervised groups of young men. Absent the domesticating influence of marriage and children, young men—especially men from working-class and poor families—were more likely to respond to the lure of the street. Akerlof noted, for instance, that substance abuse and incarceration more than doubled from 1968 to 1998. Moreover, his statistical models indicate that the growth in single men in this period was indeed linked to higher rates of substance abuse, arrests for violent crimes, and drinking.

From this research, Akerlof concluded by arguing that the contraceptive revolution played a key, albeit indirect, role in the dramatic increase in social pathology and poverty this country witnessed in the 1970s; it did so by fostering sexual license, poisoning the relations between men and women, and weakening the marital vow. In Akerlof's words: "Just at the time, about 1970, that the permanent cure to poverty seemed to be on the horizon and just at the time that women had obtained the tools to control the number and the timing of their children, single motherhood and the feminization of poverty began their long and steady rise." Furthermore, the decline in marriage caused in part by the contraceptive revolution "intensified ... the crime shock and the substance-abuse shock" that marked the 1970s and 1980s.[8]

[8] Wilcox gives the following references to Akerlof's essays: 2. George Akerlof, Janet L. Yellen, and Michael L. Katz, "An Analysis of Out-of-Wedlock Childbearing in the United States", *The Quarterly Journal of Economics* CXI (1996); George Akerlof, "Men without Children", *The Economic Journal* 108 (1998).

The Nature of the Revised Edition

I began the introduction to the first edition by affirming my belief that marriage is the rock on which the family is built and is so because it is a *person-affirming, love-enabling, life-giving*, and *sanctifying reality*. I then noted the truly incredible work of Pope John Paul II—whom I regard as the greatest champion and defender that marriage has ever had—on marriage both prior to his election as Supreme Pontiff—e.g., in plays such as *The Jeweler's Shop* (1960) and his magnificent book *Love and Responsibility* (1960), and after his election as Pope in 1978, especially in his 1982 apostolic exhortation *Familiaris consortio*, his Wednesday audiences on the "Theology of the Body", which he gave between September 9, 1979 and November 28, 1984, and his 1994 *Letter to Families*. I followed this by noting the work of the *Catechism of the Catholic Church* (promulgated by Pope John Paul II in 1992) on marriage.

In that introduction I called attention to the four volumes of the English translation of John Paul II's addresses on the Theology of the Body (TOB) published by the Daughters of St. Paul. More recently, in 2006, the Daughters of St. Paul, through their publishing arm Pauline Books and Media, have brought out a much needed new and more exact translation of these important addresses. This work, listing Pope John Paul II as author, is entitled *Man and Woman He Created Them: A Theology of the Body*, Translation, Index, and Introduction by Michael Waldstein. This new edition of the addresses on the Theology of the Body will be used throughout this new edition of *Marriage: The Rock on Which the Family Is Built*.

As in the earlier edition of this book, the first chapter, "Marriage: A Person-Affirming, Love-Enabling, Life-Giving, and Sanctifying Reality", attempts to provide an overview of the reasons why marriage is indeed the rock on which the family is built. In it I seek to provide a synthesis of the understanding of marriage in the Catholic tradition so beautifully developed by Pope John Paul II and presented in the *Catechism of the Catholic Church*. In doing so I also endeavor to formulate moral criteria for the family today. For the revised edition I have omitted the introductory material summarizing the kinds of attacks being leveled against marriage and the family at the time I wrote the first edition insofar as I have here already updated this information. I have, however, developed several of the reasons presented in the first edition to show why marriage is indeed person-affirming, love-enabling, life-giving, and sanctifying by drawing more fully on the teaching of John Paul II, particularly in his Theology of the Body, as well as on the teachings of St. Thomas, Pope Paul VI, and the *Catechism of the Catholic Church*.

The second chapter, "Marriage and the Complementarity of Male and Female", explores the complementarity of the sexes and shows how this complementarity is revealed in and is essential to the one-flesh union of man and woman in marriage. Its purpose is to show that the complementarity of male and female contributes to the meaning of marriage as person-affirming, love-enabling, life-giving, and sanctifying. In this revision I have sought in particular to show how my understanding of this complementarity harmonizes well with the thought of Pope John Paul II.

Chapter Three, devoted to an analysis of Pope Paul VI's encyclical *Humanae vitae*, is concerned primarily with the meaning of marriage as a love-enabling and life-giving reality. It is also intended to show the rich personalism at the heart of this encyclical, a personalism which, as I hope to show, has been appreciated, developed and deepened by the thought of Pope John Paul II. This true personalism is, as will be seen, utterly at odds with the pseudo-personalism—in reality, a dualism that disparages the human body and bodily life and is reminiscent of the ancient heresies of gnosticism and Manichaeanism—advanced by those who champion contraception as a morally legitimate means for deepening conjugal love and exercising responsible parenthood. Again, I have sought in this new edition to deepen arguments drawn from Paul's encyclical and John Paul II's defense of it, especially in his addresses on the Theology of the Body.

Chapter Four is an in-depth analysis of the issues raised by the ability of contemporary man to generate new human life in the laboratory. Its purpose is to show that the only way properly to respect the dignity of human life is to receive it as a "gift" crowning the one-flesh union of husband and wife in the intimacy of the marital act—to "beget" it in an act of spousal love. It is an endeavor to explore more deeply the meaning of marriage as a *life-giving* reality, one that welcomes new human life as a person equal in dignity to its progenitors and that does not dishonor it by considering it as a product inferior to its producers and subject to quality controls. I have not revised this chapter because the arguments given in it to show why in vitro fertilization is intrinsically immoral apply equally to newer methods of generating life in the laboratory, for example, cloning.

The fifth chapter is concerned with Christian marriage as a sanctifying reality, as a domestic Church. I have revised this chapter to show how the Holy Father's teaching is rooted in the teaching of Vatican Council II and have also sought to organize it more theologically.

This edition includes the following new chapters. Chapter Six, "Pope John Paul II's Catechesis on the Theology of the Body", is an attempt to show the great significance of John Paul's teaching on human sexuality in marriage and family. Chapter Seven, Pope Benedict XVI's "Teaching on Marriage and Family", presents an overview of our present Holy Father's thought on marriage, particularly as found in his first encyclical *Deus caritas est*. The Appendix of the first edition, on Pope John Paul II's "Letter to Families", is retained with minor changes.

William E. May

Marriage: A Person-Affirming, Love-Enabling, Life-Giving, and Sanctifying Reality

In this chapter I shall show that marriage, the rock upon which the family is built, is a *person-affirming, love-enabling, life-giving, and sanctifying reality*. In doing so I will develop some moral criteria for the family today.

Marriage: The Rock on Which the Family Is Built

The first and most basic moral criterion for the family of today—and of *every* day and age—is this: (1) *the family must be rooted in the marriage of one man and one woman*. This is clearly affirmed in the *Catechism of the Catholic Church*, which affirms that "a man and a woman united in marriage, together with their children, form a family. This institution is prior to any recognition by public authority, which has an obligation to recognize it. It should be considered the *normal reference point* by which the different forms of family relationship are to be evaluated" (CCC 2202, emphasis added; cf. Pope John Paul II, *Letter to Families*, no. 17). Although the reasons for it should be obvious, this basic truth, unfortunately, seems difficult for many of our contemporaries to understand. Thus I shall now try to show why this is such a basic normative truth by reflecting on the relationship between marriage and the generation of human life and by articulating other basic moral criteria for the family of today.

Marriage and the Generation of Human Life

If the human race is to continue, new human beings—new persons—must come into existence. Although it is possible today to "make" human babies in the laboratory,[1] we all know that the only bodily act through which human babies come into existence is the coital act—the genital union of a man and a woman—and that this is surely the usual way that new human beings come to be.

A human being, no matter how he comes to be, is something precious and good, a person, a being of incalculable value, worthy of respect, a bearer of inviolable rights, a being who *ought to be loved*.[2] But it is *not* good for new human life to come into existence through the random copulation of nonmarried males and females. This is not good, precisely because nonmarried males and females have failed to *capacitate* themselves, through their own free choices, to receive this life lovingly, to nourish it humanely, and to educate it in the love and service of God and man.[3]

---

[1] This subject will be explored in depth below, in Chapter Four.

[2] This truth, of course, is a matter of Catholic faith, which holds that human beings, alone of all material things, have been made in the image and likeness of God and are called to life eternal with him. But this is also a truth that can be known and defended philosophically. I cannot, of course, do so here, but I call attention to a remarkable work by the philosopher Mortimer Adler, *The Difference of Man and the Difference It Makes* (New York and Cleveland: Meridian, 1968). Adler rightly argues that "the dignity of man is the dignity of the human being as a person—a dignity not possessed by things.... the dignity of man as a person underlies the moral imperative that enjoins us never to use other human beings merely as a means, but always to respect them as ends to be served" (p. 17).

See also Karol Wojtyla (Pope John Paul II), *Love and Responsibility*, trans. H. Willetts (New York: Farrar, Straus, and Giroux, 1981; reprinted, San Francisco: Ignatius Press, 1993), p. 41 (hereafter cited as *Love and Responsibility*). "The person is the kind of good which does not admit of use and cannot be treated as an object of use and as such the means to an end.... the person is a good towards which the only proper and adequate response is love."

[3] Centuries ago St. Augustine rightly observed that one of the chief *goods* of marriage is children, who are "to be received lovingly, nourished humanely, and educated religiously", i.e., in the love and service of God and man. See his *De genesi ad literam* 9.7 (PL 34:397).

Practically all civilized societies, until recently, rightly regarded it irresponsible for unattached men and women to generate human life through their acts of fornication, and it is a sign of a new barbarism, completely opposed to the "civilization of love", that many today now assert the "right" of "live-in lovers" and of single men and women to have children, whether the fruit of their coupling or the "product" of new "reproductive" technologies.[4]

Nonmarried individuals do not have the *right* to generate human life precisely because they are not married. They refuse to give themselves unconditionally to one another and to respect the "goods" or "blessings" of marriage, among which are children and faithful conjugal love. But married men and women, precisely because they have given themselves to one another in marriage, have made themselves, as Pope Paul VI beautifully expressed matters, *fit* to generate human life.[5] By freely choosing to give themselves unreservedly to one another they have given themselves the identity of husbands and wives who *can*, together, welcome a child lovingly and give the child the home he needs if he

[4] I recognize that unmarried individuals can at times care properly for their children, and parents who become single because of widowhood or abandonment or other causes seek heroically in many instances to provide for their children, and they both need and deserve the support of the larger human community and the Church to exercise their responsibilities. But this is not the way things *ought to be*, and nothing can substitute for the home that loving spouses are able to give their children.

[5] Pope Paul VI, in *Humanae vitae*, wrote as follows: "because of its intrinsic nature the conjugal act, while uniting husband and wife in the most intimate of bonds, also *makes them* [the spouses] *fit to bring forth new life* according to laws written into their very natures as males and females" (the Latin text reads: "Etenim propter intimam suam rationem, coniugii actus dum maritum et uxorem artissimo sociat vinculo, *eos idoneos etiam facit ad novam vitam gignendam*, secundum leges in ipsa viri et mulieris natura inscriptas") (no. 12, emphasis added). The English translation of *Humanae vitae* commonly used, that provided by the Vatican, inaccurately translates the Latin by saying that the conjugal act "renders them (spouses) *capable* of generating human life. . . ." Similarly, Janet Smith, in her translation of the Latin text of *Humanae vitae*, translates *eos idoneos facit* as "makes them capable". We are *capable* of generating human life because we have genitals, and fornicators and adulterers are thus *capable* of generating life, but they are *not* fit or worthy to do so.

is "to take root" and grow. Because they have committed themselves to one another and to the "goods" or "blessings" of marriage, they have capacitated themselves to nourish the child to whom they can give life humanely and to educate the child in the love and service of God and man.

Here an analogy may be helpful. I do not have the right to diagnose sick people and prescribe medicines for them. I do not have this right because I have not freely chosen to study medicine and discipline myself so that I can acquire the knowledge and skills needed to do these tasks. But doctors, who have freely chosen to submit themselves to the discipline of studying medicine and of developing the skills necessary to practice it, do have this right. They have freely chosen to make themselves *fit* to do what doctors are supposed to do. Similarly, married men and women have, by freely choosing to marry, made themselves *fit* to do what husbands and wives are supposed to do; and among the things that husbands and wives are supposed to do is to give life to new human beings and to provide them with the home they need. Thus a second moral criterion for the family today is this: (2) *children, who are persons equal in dignity to their mothers and fathers, are to be begotten in the loving embrace of husband and wife*, and not through acts of fornication and adultery, nor are they to be "made" in the laboratory and treated as products inferior to their producers.

Marriage: A Person-affirming, Love-enabling, Life-giving, and Sanctifying Reality

1. Marriage: A Person-affirming Reality

Marriage comes into existence when a man and a woman, foreswearing all others, through an "act of irrevocable personal consent" [6] freely give themselves to one another. At the heart of the act establishing marriage is a free, self-determining choice on the

---

[6] On this, see Vatican Council II, Pastoral Constitution on the Church in the Modern World *Gaudium et spes*, no. 48.

part of the man and the woman, through which they give themselves a new and lasting identity. This man becomes this woman's *husband*, and she becomes his *wife*, and together they become *spouses*. Prior to this act of irrevocable personal consent the man and the woman are separate individuals, replaceable and substitutable in each other's lives. But in and through this act they make each other unique and irreplaceable.[7] The man and the woman are not, for each other, *replaceable and substitutable individuals* but are rather *irreplaceable and non-substitutable persons*. Thus marriage, far from being a legalistic or extrinsic limitation on the freedom of men and women or an empty formality, is indeed, as Pope John Paul II reminds us, "an interior requirement of the covenant of conjugal love which is publicly affirmed as unique and exclusive".[8]

The *Catechism of the Catholic Church*, reflecting on this crucially important matter, declares that the consent to marriage "consists in a 'human act by which the partners mutually give themselves to each other': 'I take you to be my wife'—'I take you to be my husband' [*Gaudium et spes*, no. 48; cf. *Codex Iuris Canonici*, can. 1057]. This consent that binds the spouses to each other finds its fulfillment in the two 'becoming one flesh' [Gen 2:24; cf. Mk 10:8; Eph 5:31]. The consent must be an act of the will of each of the contracting parties, free of coercion or grave external fear. No human power can substitute for this consent."[9]

Before a man and a woman marry, they are free to go their own separate ways. While each is indeed a human person and, as a person, unique and irreplaceable, they have *not* made each other unique, irreplaceable, and nonsubstitutable in their own

[7] Here the words of the late German Protestant theologian Helmut Thielicke are pertinent. He wrote: "Not uniqueness establishes the marriage, but the marriage establishes the uniqueness." *The Ethics of Sex* (New York: Harper and Row, 1963), p. 108.

[8] Pope John Paul II, apostolic exhortation *Familiaris consortio*, no. 11. John Paul II completes this sentence by writing: "in order to live in complete fidelity to the plan of God".

[9] *Catechism of the Catholic Church* (San Francisco: Ignatius Press, 1994), nos. 1627–28, hereafter cited as CCC.

lives. Before they get married they may say that they love one another—and they undoubtedly do. Before they marry, they have a special kind of human friendship love, one that *aspires* to full union, one that *aspires* to marriage and to conjugal love, but they are still at liberty to change their minds and live their own lives independently of one another. They have not yet *established* their uniqueness, their irreplaceability, their nonsubstitutability. But once they have given their irrevocable, personal consent to marriage, they have done something that they cannot undo. For they have, through their own free and self-determining choices, given to themselves and to one another a new kind of identity, and nothing they subsequently can do can change this identity. They simply cannot *unspouse* themselves. They cannot make themselves *to be* ex-husbands and ex-wives any more than I can make myself to be an ex-father to the children whom I have begotten. I may be a bad father, a terrible father, but I am still my children's *father*. I may be a bad husband, a terrible husband, but I am still my wife's *husband* and she is my *wife*. I have made her irreplaceable and nonsubstitutable in my life, and she has made me irreplaceable and nonsubstitutable in hers. We have freely chosen to unite our lives, for better, for worse, for richer, for poorer, in sickness and in health, until *death* do us part.

From this we can see that the *indissolubility* of marriage is ontologically grounded, for it is rooted in the very *being* of the man and the woman, in their freely chosen *identity* as husbands and wives, as persons made irreplaceable and nonsubstitutable in each other's life. The truth that marriage, as a person-affirming reality, is established in and through the free, self-determining choice of the man and the woman is clearly indicated in Scripture. In the second account of the creation of man and of woman, and of marriage, which we find in the second chapter of Genesis, we read that the first man, on awakening from the deep sleep into which God had put him when he fashioned the first woman from his ribs, exclaimed, "This at last is bone of my bones and flesh of my flesh. . . . For this reason a man shall leave father and mother and cleave to his wife, and the two shall become one flesh" (Gen 2:23–24).

Pope John Paul II's commentary on this passage is of great importance:

> The formulation of Genesis 2:24 itself indicates not only that human beings, created as man and woman, have been created for unity, but also that precisely this *unity, through which they become "one flesh," has from the beginning the character of a union that derives from a choice.* We read, in fact, "A man will leave his father and his mother and unite with his wife." While the man, by virtue of generation, belongs "by nature" to his father and mother, "he unites," by contrast, with his wife (or she with her husband) by choice. The text of Genesis 2:24 defines this character of the conjugal bond in reference to the first man and the first woman, but at the same time it does so also in the perspective of man's earthly future as a whole. In his own time, therefore, Christ was to appeal to this text as equally relevant in his age. Since they are formed in the image of God also inasmuch as they form an authentic communion of persons, the first man and the first woman must constitute the beginning and model of that communion for all men and women who in any period unite with each other so intimately that they are "one flesh." The body, which through its own masculinity and femininity helps the two ("a help similar to himself") from the beginning to find themselves in a communion of persons [see *Gaudium et Spes*, 24.3], becomes in a particular way the constitutive element of their union when they become husband and wife. This takes place, however, through a reciprocal choice. The choice is what establishes the conjugal covenant between the persons, who become "one flesh" only based on this choice.[10]

Indeed, it is precisely because marriage, as a person-affirming reality, is rooted in the *irrevocable* choice of the man and the woman *to be* spouses, that our Lord not only expressly condemned divorce ("let no man separate what God has joined", Mk 10:9), but also said that any divorce that might possibly take place had no effect

---

[10] Pope John Paul II, *Man and Woman He Created Them: A Theology of the Body* (hereafter *Man and Woman*): A New Translation Based on the Archives. Translation, Introduction, and Index by Michael Waldstein (Boston: Pauline Books and Media, 2006), 10.3, p. 168. The numerals 10.3 refer to the tenth address in the Theology of the Body series and to the second paragraph in that address. This way of referring to the text of John Paul II's addresses will be used throughout.

whatever on the bond of marriage itself ("whoever divorces his wife and marries another commits adultery against her; and the woman who divorces her husband and marries another commits adultery", Mk 10:11–12).

Thus the *Catechism of the Catholic Church* teaches, "*the marriage bond* has been established by God himself. . . . This bond, which results from the free human act of the spouses and their consummation of the marriage, is a reality, henceforth irrevocable, and gives rise to a covenant guaranteed by God's fidelity." [11]

2. Marriage: A Love-enabling Reality

Marriage is not only a person-affirming reality, but it is also a *love-enabling* reality, for it enables husbands and wives to give to one another the unique and special kind of love that we call spousal or conjugal love, one quite different from other kinds of human love. Other kinds of human love—love of neighbor, love of one's children, love of one's enemies—are inclusive, not exclusive. We are to love all our neighbors, all our children, all our enemies. But the love of husband and wife is absolutely unique and different. It is first of all absolutely *exclusive*. A husband can love no other woman as he loves his wife, and a wife can love no other man as she loves her husband. Yet conjugal love, while exclusive, by no means locks husband and wife into an *égoisme à deux*. To the contrary, it enables them, precisely because of their unique and exclusive love for one another, to love other persons more fully and deeply.

Vatican Council II, in its Pastoral Constitution on the Church in the Modern World *Gaudium et spes* (nos. 49–50) and Pope Paul VI in his encyclical *Humanae vitae* (no. 9) describe conjugal love as a love that is human, total, faithful and exclusive until death, and fecund or fertile. It is, in other words, a love that differs from other kinds of human love because it includes the whole of the other person as a human, sexual, procreative being, sexually complementary in nature. Pope John Paul II, in a

[11] CCC 1639.

magnificent passage in his apostolic exhortation *Familiaris consortio*, which the *Catechism of the Catholic Church* makes its own, beautifully describes the nature of this love:

> Conjugal love involves a totality, in which all the elements of the person enter—appeal of the body and instinct, power of feeling and affectivity, aspiration of the spirit and of the will. It aims at a deeply personal unity, a unity that, beyond union in one flesh, leads to forming one heart and soul; it demands *indissolubility* and *faithfulness* in definitive mutual giving; and it is open to *fertility*.[12]

As Vatican Council II teaches us, marriage is "the intimate community of life and of conjugal love".[13] The institution of marriage *protects and defends* conjugal love, which is the *life-giving* or animating principle of marriage. *Conjugal love*, we can rightly say, *constitutes the personal reality that the institution of marriage confirms, protects, and sanctions before God and man.*[14] The first act of conjugal love is the act of irrevocable personal consent whereby a man and woman, by freely giving themselves to one another as husband and wife, establish their marriage, a *person-affirming reality*. This person-affirming reality enables husbands and wives to *give* to each other the love that is unique and proper to them, *conjugal love*, because only spouses can give love of this kind and what makes a man and a woman *to be spouses* is their marriage. Even if this love should, tragically, be actually withdrawn as the spouses' life together unfolds, it remains as the *life-giving principle* and *intrinsic*

---

[12] *Familiaris consortio*, no. 13; cited in CCC 1643.

[13] *Gaudium et spes*, no. 48.

[14] This is the truth beautifully developed at Vatican Council II in *Gaudium et spes*, nos. 48–49. Excellent commentaries on these important texts are given by Francisco Gil Hellín and Ramón García de Haro. See Francisco Gil Hellín, "El Matrimonio: Amor e Institucion", in *Cuestiones Fundamentales sobre Matrimonio y Familia*, ed. A. Sarmiento et al. (Pamplona: EUNSA, 1980), pp. 231–45, hereafter cited as "El matrimonío", and "El lugar proprio del amor conyugal en la estructura del matrimonio segun la 'Gaudium et spes'", in *Annales Valentinos* 6.11 (1980), hereafter cited as "El lugar proprio del amor". See Ramón García de Haro, *Marriage and Family in the Documents of the Magisterium*, trans. from the Italian by William E. May (San Francisco: Ignatius Press, 1993), pp. 234–56, hereafter cited as *Marriage and Family*.

requirement of marriage. Husbands and wives are under an obligation to *give* this love to each other because they have freely committed themselves to give it; moreover, they *can* give this love because their marriage enables them to do so. Thus a third basic moral criterion for families, which are rooted in the reality of marriage, is this: (3) *husbands and wives must give to each other the gift of conjugal love and deepen it throughout their lives.* By freely consenting to give themselves to one another in marriage, they have established each other as non-substitutable and irreplaceable persons and, by doing so, have capacitated themselves to give one another *conjugal love.* This love, "ratified by mutual faith", must be "indissolubly faithful amidst the prosperities and adversities of both body and soul".[15] Only if they subsequently do what they are now capable of doing will a "civilization of love" be possible.

3. Marriage: A Life-giving Reality

That marriage is a *life-giving* reality is clearly brought out in the "creation narratives" of Genesis 1 and 2. Chapter 1, attributed to the Priestly/Elohist tradition, indeed declares: "God created man in his own image; in the divine image he created him; male and female he created them. God blessed them, saying 'Be fertile and multiply'" (Gen 1:27–28). And in Chapter 2, attributed to the later Yahwist tradition, we read that a man leaves his father and mother and cleaves to his wife so that the two "will be one flesh" (Gen 2:24). Commenting on the text from Genesis 2, John Paul II has the following to say: "The unity about which Genesis 2:24 speaks ('and the two will be one flesh') is without doubt the unity that is expressed and realized in the conjugal act. The biblical formulation, so extremely concise and simple, indicates sex, that is, masculinity and femininity, as that characteristic of man— male and female—that allows them, when they become one flesh, to place their whole humanity at the same time under the blessing of fruitfulness" (*Man and Woman*, 10.2, p. 167).

[15] *Gaudium et spes*, no. 49.

That marriage is life-giving was a point made to some extent in reflecting on marriage and the generation of human life. Here I will relate marriage as a life-giving reality to marriage as a love-enabling reality by reflecting on the nature of conjugal love and the meaning of the conjugal act. Any love between two persons is impossible unless there is some common good that binds them together, and man's capacity for love depends on his willingness to seek a good together with others and to subordinate himself to that good for the sake of others or to others for the sake of that good.

This principle is true of every form of human love and is central to a "civilization of love". But in marriage this principle is revealed in a special and unique way. For in marriage, and in marriage alone, two people, a man and a woman, are united in such a way that they become "one flesh", i.e., the common subject, as it were, of a sexual life. To ensure that one of them does not become for the other nothing more than an object of use, a means to the attainment of some selfish end, they must share the same end or common good. "Such an end, where marriage is concerned"—so Pope John Paul II, writing as the philosopher Karol Wojtyla, has said—"is the procreation and education of children, the future generation, a family, and, at the same time, the continual ripening of the relationship between two people, in all the areas of activity which conjugal life includes. These objective purposes of marriage create in principle the possibility of love and exclude the possibility of treating a person as a means to an end and as an object for use." [16]

In other words, in getting married a man and a woman not only give to themselves the irrevocable identity of husband and wife but also pledge to one another that they will honor and foster the "goods" or "blessings" of marriage, namely, the procreation and education of children and steadfast faithful love.

The reality of these "goods" is beautifully revealed in the marital or conjugal act, for which marriage also capacitates the spouses. The conjugal act is indeed a very specific and special kind of act.

[16] *Love and Responsibility*, p. 30.

It is, first of all, an act that manifests uniquely and fittingly the sexual complementarity of husband and wife as male and female. I believe that we can rightly regard human sexuality as a *giving and a receiving*. It is a giving and a receiving for both males and females. However, males and females express their sexuality—their giving and receiving—in complementary ways: the male gives in a receiving sort of way, while the female receives in a giving sort of way. It is not that the male is active and the female passive. There is activity on the part of both, but the man, precisely because of the kind of sexual being that he is, gives in a receiving sort of way while the female, precisely because she is the kind of sexual being she is, receives in a giving sort of way. Their sexuality is, as we shall see more fully in Chapter Two, complementary in this way: male sexuality is an emphasis on giving in a receiving sort of way, whereas female sexuality is an emphasis on receiving in a giving sort of way.

This is illustrated in a striking way in the marital or conjugal act. In this act the husband gives himself to his wife by entering into her body, her person, and in doing so he receives her into himself, while she, in receiving him bodily into herself, gives to him the gift of herself.

To understand the significance of the conjugal or marital act it is, secondly, most important to recognize that the marital act is not simply a genital act between a man and a woman who "happen" to be married. It is, rather, an act participating in the marriage itself and one made possible only because of the marriage: marriage, in short, enables husband and wife to engage in the marital act. I hope now to show why this is true.

Nonmarried men and women are capable of engaging in *genital* acts because they are endowed with genitals. But when nonmarried men and women have sex, they do not, and *cannot, give* themselves to each other and *receive* each other. The man cannot give himself to the woman in a receiving sort of way, nor can she receive him in a giving sort of way. They cannot do so precisely because they are *not* married. They have refused to make each other irreplaceable and nonsubstitutable persons; they have refused to make each other *spouses*. Their sexual act, therefore, does *not* unite two irreplaceable and nonsubstitutable persons; it merely *joins* two individuals who remain *in principle* replaceable, substitutable, disposable. There can be, between them, no true giving in a receiving sort of way or receiving in a giving sort of way. Their sexual act is, in fact, a lie.[17] They do not *give* their bodies, their persons, to each other; rather they *lend* their bodies to each other.

But husbands and wives, who have freely chosen to give themselves the identity of irreplaceable and nonsubstitutable spouses, are capable of the conjugal or spousal act—of giving in a receiving sort of way and receiving in a giving sort of way. And they are capable of doing so precisely because of their marriage. Thus the conjugal act, precisely as *conjugal*, is an act that participates in their marriage, which, as we have seen, comes into existence when the man gives himself unreservedly to the woman in a receiving sort of way and when she in turn unreservedly receives him in a giving sort of way. The marital act is, therefore, one that respects the "goods" or "blessings" of marriage, i.e., the goods of children and of faithful conjugal love. As marital, therefore, it is an act (1) open to the communication of conjugal love and (2) open to the gift of new human life.

If the husband, in choosing to have sex with his wife, refuses to give himself in a receiving sort of way but rather seeks simply to use his wife to satisfy his sexual desires, he is not, in truth, engaging in the conjugal act, nor would his wife be doing so were she to refuse to receive him in a giving sort of way.

A remarkable passage in Pope Paul VI's encyclical *Humanae vitae* brings out this important truth. In it he said that everyone will recognize that a conjugal act (and here he was using the expression in a purely descriptive sense as a *sexual* act between a man and woman who merely happen to be married and not in its moral sense as an act participating in marriage itself) imposed upon one of the spouses with no consideration of his or her condition or legitimate desires, "is not a true act of love", inasmuch as it "opposes what the moral order rightly requires from

---

[17] On this see Pope John Paul II, *Familiaris consortio*, no. 11.

spouses".[18] It is, in reality, not a true conjugal act, for it violates one of the essential *goods* of marriage, namely, conjugal love, and precisely because it does so it does not inwardly participate in the marriage itself. It is rather an act of spousal abuse.

Indeed, as Pope John Paul II has rightly reminded us, a husband can in a true sense commit adultery with his own wife if he simply uses her as a means to gratify his lust without any concern for her well-being (*Man and Woman*, 43.2). In saying this, the Holy Father simply reaffirmed the Catholic tradition. After all, a husband can look lustfully at his wife and commit adultery with her in his heart, and if *this* is what he intends in having sex with her, he is committing adultery in the flesh as well. This was the common teaching of the Fathers of the Church and of St. Thomas Aquinas, who said that if a man has intercourse with his wife, not caring that she is his wife but simply a woman whom he can use to satisfy lust, he sins mortally.[19] Marriage does not enable men and women to engage in lustful sexual acts—their sinful hearts do this—but it does enable them to engage in the conjugal or marital act.

Because it participates in the blessings or goods of marriage, the conjugal act is also one that is open to the gift of new life. Conjugal love, as we have seen, is a love that is not only human, total, faithful and exclusive until death, but *fertile*. Conjugal love is procreative in nature. Indeed, as the *Catechism of the Catholic Church* says, "a child does not come from outside as something added on to the mutual love of the spouses, but springs *from the very heart of that mutual giving*, as its fruit and fulfillment."[20] The conjugal act, which uniquely expresses conjugal love, is thus the sort of act meant to welcome new human life, a wondrous and

---

[18] Pope Paul VI, *Humanae vitae*, 13: "People rightly understand that a conjugal act imposed on a spouse, with no consideration given to the condition of the spouse or to the legitimate desires of the spouse, is not a true act of love. They understand that such an act opposes what the right moral order rightly requires from spouses."

[19] On this see Thomas Aquinas, *Summa theologiae*, supplement to part III, q. 49, a. 6.

[20] CCC 2366.

surpassing good. As Jesus said, "Let the little children come to me and do not hinder them" (Lk 18:16).

Hence, just as husbands and wives violate their marriage and render their sexual union *nonmarital* if, in choosing to unite sexually, they deliberately repudiate conjugal love or the unitive meaning of the conjugal act, so too they violate their marriage and render their sexual union *nonmarital* if, in freely choosing to unite sexually, they deliberately repudiate its life-giving or procreative meaning.[21] This brings us to a fourth moral criterion for families: (4) *spouses ought not, either in anticipation of their marital union, while engaging in it, or during the development of its natural consequences, propose, either as end or means, to impede procreation.*[22] If they choose to do this, they are setting their hearts, their wills, against the good of human life in its transmission. Their choice is anti-life. Moreover, if they do choose to do this, their sexual union is no longer truly a conjugal act, for it is not only anti-life but anti-love—they do not truly "give" themselves unreservedly to one another.[23]

Since the life of a human person must be respected from its beginning, a fifth moral criterion for families immediately ensues,

---

[21] *Humanae vitae*, no. 13. In this remarkable passage Pope Paul first notes, as we have seen, that people easily understand why it is contrary to the moral order for one spouse to "impose" a conjugal act on the other with no consideration being given to the condition or legitimate desires of the other. He continues by saying: "To be consistent, then, if they reflect further, they should acknowledge that it is necessarily true that an act of mutual love that impairs the capacity of bringing forth life contradicts both the divine plan that established the nature of the conjugal bond and also the will of the first Author of human life."

[22] This is precisely the definition of contraception found in *Humanae vitae*, no. 14. Contraception includes "every action, which either in anticipation of the conjugal act, or in its accomplishment, or in the development of its natural consequences, proposes [*intendat* is the Latin term employed], either as end or as means, to impede procreation [the Latin text reads: *ut procreatio impediatur*]". This matter will be taken up at greater depth in Chapter Three.

[23] For a detailed development of this, see Germain Grisez, John Finnis, Joseph Boyle, and William E. May, "'Every Marital Act Ought to Be Open to New Life': Toward a Clarification", in *The Thomist* 52 (1988): 365–426; reprinted in the book by the same authors and John Ford, S.J., *The Teaching of "Humanae Vitae": A Defense* (San Francisco: Ignatius Press, 1988). Hereafter cited as Grisez et al., *Every Marital Act*. See also Chapters Three and Four below.

namely, (5) *it is always gravely wrong freely to choose to abort unborn babies.*

Husbands and wives are to be *responsible* parents, and there can be no true contradiction between their obligation to respect the procreative good of marriage and the fostering of conjugal love.[24] There may be serious reasons for a married couple to limit the number of their children and perhaps to refrain from having any. But in exercising their responsibilities in this matter they ought not freely choose to set their hearts against the good of human life in its transmission; rather, they should freely choose to respect the fertile cycles of the wife.[25] Thus a sixth moral criterion for the family today is this: (6) *husbands and wives must learn to foster conjugal love by respecting the wife's fertility and by abstaining from the marital act when there is good reason to do so.* Loving husbands and wives are connaturally disposed to honor these criteria and find their violation repugnant. They do so because these criteria naturally flow from the meaning of marriage as a *life-giving reality* rooted in conjugal love, a love open to good of human life.

4. Marriage: A Sanctifying Reality

The Church has always taught that God is the author of marriage. The creation accounts in the first chapters of Genesis are narratives not only of the creation of the universe, not only of the creation of man, male and female, but also of the creation of *marriage.* God is the Author, the Creator, both of human nature and the nature of marriage. But God is also the one who has

---

[24] Cf. *Gaudium et spes,* no. 52.

[25] It is not possible to enter into a discussion of the vast differences between respect for human fertility (natural family planning) and contraception (the free choice to impede procreation) here. However, as Pope John Paul II has rightly noted, there is a "radical difference, both anthropological and moral, between contraception and recourse to the rhythms of the cycle" as ways of regulating conception, a difference ultimately rooted in "irreconcilable concepts of human sexuality and of the human person". *Familiaris consortio,* no. 32. On this matter see the article by Grisez et al. referred to in note 23 above.

willed to enter into a covenant of love with human persons; he is the source of sanctifying grace, which enables us to share his divine nature, just as his only begotten Son, in becoming man, shares our human nature. Nature is for grace; creation is for covenant.

God has willed our human nature to be the *kind* of nature that it is—the nature of persons endowed with intelligence and free choice—precisely so that we would be free to accept his offer of grace and to enter into an everlasting covenant with him. He cannot give his own life to nonrational creatures likes dogs or cats or chimpanzees simply because these creatures of his are not inwardly open to receive this surpassing gift. Nor could he become incarnate in creatures of this kind. But he *can* give us his very own life because he has made us to be the kind of beings capable of receiving it. And he *can*—and *has*—become incarnate in human flesh in the person of his only begotten Son, precisely in order to redeem us from sin and enable us to become fully the beings he wills us to be: his own children, his sons and daughters, members of his own divine family.

Similarly, God has given the human reality of marriage the *nature* it has because he wills to integrate it into his divine plan and to make it a means of holiness, of sanctification. And he has so integrated it into his loving and wise plan of human redemption in the life, death, and resurrection of his Son, who raised the marriages of Christians to the dignity of a sacrament of the new and everlasting covenant.

Recall that the prophets of the Old Testament (Hosea, Jeremiah, Isaiah, Ezekiel) fittingly used the human reality of marriage as a symbol of the loving union or covenant between God and his chosen people. His Son, Jesus, is the supreme prophet, the One who fully reveals to us the mystery of God's love for mankind, the One who brings into being the new and eternal covenant of God's love for us. And in the New Testament Jesus is portrayed as the Bridegroom par excellence, the One who gives his life for his spotless bride the Church. Moreover, in the New Testament we read that the human reality of marriage symbolizes the bridal union of Christ and his Church; this is the "great mystery" to which marriage points (cf. Eph 5:23ff.).

In addition, the marriage of Christians, of those who "marry in the Lord", not only points to or symbolizes the life-giving, love-giving, grace-giving, and sanctifying union of Christ and the Church, but it also inwardly participates in this bridal union and makes it efficaciously present in the world. Christians have already, by baptism, become "new" creatures in Christ: they have become, through Christ, with Christ, and in Christ, members of the divine family, children of his Father, led by his Spirit. As a result, when Christians unite sexually with others they do so not as isolated individuals but as members of Christ's living body the Church. Should they do so outside of marriage, they not only act immorally but desecrate the body of Christ (cf. 1 Cor 6:15–17). But when they give themselves to each other in marriage, which is to be honored in every way (cf. Heb 13:4), they marry "in the Lord". Precisely because Christian husbands and wives are *already*, through baptism, "new" creatures, members of the household of God, their marital union inwardly participates in the grace-giving, sanctifying, redemptive union of Christ and his Church. Their marriage is a sacrament of sanctifying grace.

Thus the marriage of Christians is a sanctifying reality. It enables Christian husbands and wives to love one another with a redemptive, sanctifying love, for their human conjugal love has been graced by Christ himself and merges the divine with the human. In forming a communion of persons, Christian husbands and wives indeed bring into existence the "domestic church", the "church in miniature".[26] The Christian family, therefore, has a specific and original role to play within the larger Church. Its mission is to participate in a unique way in the redemptive work of Christ. Its task, as Pope John Paul II has so well expressed it, is to be fully what it *is*, i.e., a believing and evangelizing community, a community in dialogue with God, a community serving others by transforming the world through Christ's redemptive love. It is a

[26] On this see Vatican Council II, Dogmatic Constitution on the Church *Lumen gentium*, no. 11; Decree on the Lay Apostolate *Apostolicam actuositatem*, no. 11; *Familiaris consortio*, no. 49; CCC 1655–58. This matter will be taken up in depth in Chapter Five.

community that participates in the prophetic, priestly, and kingly mission of Christ.[27]

Marriage, by the will of God, has been made a sacrament of sanctifying grace, capable of helping Christian husbands and wives answer God's call to be holy, enabling them to participate in a unique and indispensable way in the redemptive work of Christ. Thus a seventh moral criterion for the Christian family today is this: (7) *the Christian family must carry out its mission as the domestic Church and participate in Christ's redemptive work.* This is a subject that will be explored in greater depth in Chapter Five.

Marriage and Family as Serving Life and the Human Community

1. Parents' Obligations toward Their Children

Husbands and wives are called not only to receive life lovingly, but to nourish it humanely and to educate it in the love and service of God, and their marriage *capacitates* them for these tasks too. This is an eighth moral criterion for the family: (8) *parents have the duty, and the right, to educate their own children.* This duty and the right corresponding to it flow from the very nature of fatherly and motherly love, a love that is fulfilled "in the task of education as it completes and perfects its service to life".[28]

The duty of parents to educate their children encompasses the following elements. First of all, parents (a) need to help their children acquire a sense of values, in particular a correct attitude toward material goods, which are intended to serve persons, who must always be considered as more precious for what they *are*

---

[27] On this see Pope John Paul II, *Familiaris consortio*, nos. 49–64; see also his *Letter to Families*.

[28] *Familiaris consortio*, no. 36. See also CCC 1653, where we read: "The fruitfulness of conjugal love extends to the fruits of the moral, spiritual, and supernatural life that parents hand on to their children by education. Parents are the principal and first educators of their children. In this sense the fundamental task of marriage and family is to be at the service of life."

than for what they *have*. Second (b) they must help their children
learn that they must cultivate virtues if they are to be truly the
persons they are meant to be, and particularly today, in a world
that is hostile to the "civilization of love", the virtues of justice
and love. Finally (c), they need to educate their children in the
area of human sexuality, leading them to appreciate the beauty of
their sexuality and the human significance of and need for the
virtue of chastity, a virtue that enables them to come into possession of their sexual desires and urges and not to be possessed
by them, a virtue that capacitates them to *give themselves away in
love to others.*[29]

The work of parents in educating their own children is indispensable. "It is not an exaggeration", Pope John Paul II has said,
"to reaffirm that the life of nations, of states, and of international
organizations 'passes' through the family.... [Indeed] *through the
family passes the primary current of the civilization of love*, which finds
therein its 'social foundations'."[30]

Parents share their educational mission with other individuals
or institutions, such as the Church and the State. But it is imperative that the mission of education respect the *principle of subsid-
iarity*. This implies the legitimacy and indeed the need of giving
help to parents, but it is limited by their right as the *primary educators* of their children. Indeed "all other participants in the process of education are only able to carry out their responsibilities
in the name of the parents, with their consent and, to a certain degree,
with their authorization."[31] Thus a ninth moral criterion for the
family today is this: (9) *Church and state must both honor the primary
right of parents as educators of their children and cooperate with them in
this educative task.*

Children learn from the example given to them perhaps even
more than from what is said to them. Thus, in connection with
the right and duty of parents to educate their children, it seems

---

[29] On this see *Familiaris consortio*, no. 37. An excellent treatment of chastity is
provided by Karol Wojtyla in *Love and Responsibility*. See also my Synthesis Series
booklet, *The Nature and Meaning of Chastity* (Chicago: Franciscan Herald Press, 1977).

[30] *Letter to Families*, no. 15.

[31] Ibid., no. 16.

to me that the following is sound advice: one of the best gifts that a husband can give his wife is to love her children and, vice versa, one of the best gifts a wife can give her husband is to love his children. And one of the best gifts a father can give his children is to love their mother, and vice versa.

2. The Family's Service to Society

By nature and vocation the family rooted in the marriage of one man and one woman is open to other families and to society. The obligation of the family to serve society and the wider human community is, indeed, not something added on to or extrinsic to the family, but is rooted in its *being*. The family has vital and organic links with society, since it is its foundation and nourishes it continually through its service to life; it is from the family that citizens come to birth and it is within the family that they find the first school of the social virtues that are the animating principle of the existence and development of society itself.[32]

The "first and fundamental contribution" of the family to society is "the very experience of communion and sharing that should characterize the family's daily life".[33] By becoming what it is meant to be, the family is the first and most efficacious school of sociality, through the spontaneous gratuity of the relationships among its members, which takes place through their cordial welcoming of each other, their disinterested availability, their generous service, their deep solidarity.

The family contributes to the good of society by works of social service, especially by means of hospitality, by opening "the door of one's home and still more of one's heart to the pleas of one's brothers and sisters".[34]

A tenth moral criterion for the family today, therefore, is: (10) *the family must serve society by works of social service, in particular, by hospitality to others.*

[32] *Familiaris consortio,* no. 42. See also CCC 2207.
[33] *Familiaris consortio,* no. 42.
[34] Ibid., no. 44.

Precisely because the family is the first school in the "civilization of love" and contributes so efficaciously to the well-being of society, there is a corresponding obligation on the part of society and the state to recognize and respect the role of the family in the development of society. Thus an eleventh moral criterion for the family of today is this: (11) *society and the state must serve the family; they must make it possible for it to obtain the helps of which it has need and recognize the rights of the family in a formal way.*[35]

Since, unfortunately, the rights of the family are today threatened and ignored by many states and societies, families themselves "must be the first to take steps to see that laws and institutions of the state not only do not offend but support and positively defend the rights and duties of families".[36] Families must become protagonists of "family politics" and assume "responsibility for transforming society". This gives us a twelfth moral criterion for the family of today: (12) *families must defend their rights and duties.* Pope John Paul II adds:

> In connection with this matter, there is great need today to respect the rights of women and, in particular, of mothers. There is, of course, "no doubt that the equal dignity and responsibility of men and women fully justifies women's access to public functions." Nonetheless, while it must be recognized that women have the same right as men to perform various public functions, society must be structured in such a way that wives and mothers are *not in practice compelled* to work outside the home, and that their families can live and prosper in a dignified way even when they themselves devote their full time to their own family. . . . [T]he mentality which honors women more for their work outside the home than for their work within the family must be overcome. This requires that men should truly esteem and love women with total respect for their personal dignity, and that

[35] On this cf. ibid. See also the *Charter of the Rights of the Family* presented by the Holy See to All Persons, Institutions and Authorities Concerned with the Mission of the Family in Today's World, October 23, 1983, and also CCC 2210–11.

[36] *Familiaris consortio*, no. 44.

society should create and develop conditions favoring work in the home.[37]

A thirteenth moral criterion for the family today, therefore, can be expressed as follows: (13) *Society must respect the contribution made by mothers who choose to remain at home and care for their children, and secure its just compensation.*

The "Good of the Spouses" (*Bonum Coniugum*)

The truth that marriage is a *sanctifying reality* is magnificently deepened by the teaching of the postconciliar Church regarding the "good of the spouses" or the *bonum coniugum*. It will thus be helpful here to reflect on the meaning of this "good".

The very first canon on marriage in the 1983 *Code of Canon Law* declares: "The matrimonial covenant, by which a man and a woman establish between themselves a partnership for the whole of life, is by its nature ordered toward the good of the spouses and the procreation and education of offspring." [38] And the *Catechism of the Catholic Church* reaffirms this in its opening paragraph devoted to the sacrament of matrimony.[39] Thus the Church today identifies as the principal ends of marriage both the procreation and education of children and what she calls the "good of the spouses", the *bonum coniugum*, and in fact the Code of Canon Law and the Catechism name this end first.

The expression "good of the spouses", however, is very recent and was first used to designate an end of marriage in the revised

[37] Ibid., no. 23. In his *Letter to Families* Pope John Paul II had the following to say on this topic: "The 'toil' of a woman who, having given birth to a child, nourishes and cares for that child and devotes herself to its upbringing, particularly in the early years, is so great as to be comparable to any professional work. This ought to be clearly stated and upheld, no less than any other labor right. Motherhood, because of all the hard work it entails, should be recognized as giving the right to financial benefits at least equal to those of other kinds of work undertaken in order to support the family during such a delicate phase of its life" (17).

[38] *Code of Canon Law*, canon 1055, par. 1.

[39] CCC 1601.

Code of Canon Law in 1983. It was not explicitly identified as such either by Vatican Council II[40] or by Pope John Paul II in his 1981 apostolic exhortation *Familiaris consortio*. Nor have theologians given much thought to the meaning of this good.[41] But canon lawyers have debated its meaning to considerable extent, and a splendid doctoral study in canon law by Dominic Kimengich provides a tentative formulation of the essential content of this good. According to him it consists in

> the growth and maturing of the spouses as persons, through the aids, comforts, and consolations, but also through the demands and hardships, of conjugal life, when lived according to God's plan. The full view of the scope and content of the "good of the spouses" emerges when we recall that the spouses are called to eternal life, which is the one definitive *bonum* of the spouses.[42]

[40] Vatican Council II did use the expression "good of the spouses" in *Gaudium et spes*, no. 48, but not in the sense of an end of marriage. In no. 48 it declared: "for the good of the spouses, of the children, and of society, this sacred bond [*sacrum vinculum*] no longer depends on human decision alone."

[41] In fact, the expression "good of the spouses" (*bonum coniugum*) is not even mentioned in the following very excellent works on marriage, faithful to the Magisterium, published after the publication of the 1983 revision of the *Code of Canon Law*: Peter Elliott, *What God Has Joined: The Sacramentality of Marriage* (New York: Alba House, 1989); Agostino Sarmiento, *El Matrimonio* (Pamplona: EUNSA, 1998); Francisco Gil Hellín, *El Matrimonio y la Vida Conyugal* (Valencia: Edicep C.B., 1995); Germain Grisez, Chapter 8. "Marriage and Sexual Acts", in his *Living a Christian Life*, a book-length treatment of marriage in vol. 2 of his *The Way of the Lord Jesus* (Quincy, IL: Franciscan Press, 1993), pp. 553–751; Ramón García de Haro, *Marriage and Family in the Documents of the Magisterium*. Some theologians, e.g., Antonio Miralles, identify the "good of the spouses" with the old good of "mutual assistance" and discuss it only very briefly. See his *El Matrimonio* (Pamplona: EUNSA, 1993), p. 102. This view, however, is hardly correct. Dominic Kimengich and Cormac Burke offer serious criticism of this opinion, also championed by many canonists.

[42] Dominic Kimengich, *The Bonum Coniugum: A Canonical Appraisal* (Rome: Pontificiu Athenaeum Santae Crocis, 1997), p. 204. Kimengich's thesis was directed by Cormac Burke, a canonist and theologian who has himself written extensively and well on the meaning of the "good of the spouses". See Burke, "The *Bonum Coniugum* and the *Bonum Prolis*: Ends or Properties of Marriage?" *The Jurist* 49 (1989) 704–13.

Kimengich here suggests that the *bonum coniugum* is, in the last analysis, found in the sanctification of the spouses. I believe that this is true, and thus I will try to show that the "good of the spouses" ultimately consists in the holiness or sanctification that husbands and wives are meant to attain precisely in and through their married life, and that the teaching of Pope Pius XI in his 1930 encyclical *Casti connubii* is central in understanding this.

To show this it is imperative to consult the "sources" for canon 1055, where the "good of the spouses" was first identified as an essential end of marriage. The Pontifical Commission for the Interpretation of the Code of Canon Law in its annotated version of the code in 1989 enumerated these sources; in my opinion the most central of these is the teaching of Pius XI in *Casti connubii*.[43] But before looking at the thought of Pius XI let us look at the other sources the commission identified. Three are passages from Vatican Council II, and these passages are also very important in showing that the "good of the spouses" ultimately consists in their sanctification. The first is the chapter of its Dogmatic Constitution on the Church devoted to the theme, "The Universal Call to Holiness";[44] the second is from the same constitution identifying marriage as a specific vocation to holiness,[45] and the third is found in the Council's presentation of the dignity of marriage and the family in the Pastoral Constitution on the Church in the Modern World, where it declared that husbands and wives "increasingly further their own perfection and their mutual sanctification" by fulfilling their conjugal and family roles.[46]

Another source is a passage from Pope Pius XII's 1951 Address to the Italian Union of Midwives in which he spoke of the "personal perfecting of the spouses" as a "secondary end" of marriage.[47] Finally, the commission referred to the passage in Pius XI's *Casti connubii*, where he declared that married love "demands not

---

[43] *Pontificia Commissio per Interpretationem Codicis Iuris Canonici, Codex Iuris Canonici* (Vatican City: Libreria Editrice Vaticana, 1989).

[44] See *Lumen gentium*, nos. 39–42.

[45] Ibid.

[46] *Gaudium et spes*, no. 48. See also *Apostolicam actuositatem*, no. 11.

[47] Ibid.

only mutual aid but must have as its *primary purpose* (emphasis added) that man and wife help each other day by day *in forming and perfecting themselves in the interior life* [emphasis in original], so that through their partnership in life they may advance ever more and more in virtue, and above all that they may grow in true love toward God and their neighbor".[48] I believe that this statement of Pius XI, together with one immediately following it, is the major source of the teaching that the "good of the spouses" is an essential end of marriage.

Surprisingly, the Pontifical Commission did not call attention to the paragraph in *Casti connubii* immediately following this citation. This is surprising because this text is of utmost importance in understanding the *bonum coniugum* as an end of marriage and how this end is intrinsically related to the spouses' vocation to holiness precisely as spouses. In it Pope Pius XI declared:

> This inward molding of husband and wife, this determined effort to perfect each other, can in a very real sense, as the Roman Catechism teaches, be said to be the chief reason and purpose of matrimony, provided matrimony be looked at not in the restricted sense as instituted for the proper conception and education of the child, but more widely as the blending of life as a whole and the mutual interchange and sharing thereof.[49]

The text of the *Roman Catechism* (popularly known as *The Catechism of the Council of Trent*) to which Pius refers reads as follows: "The first reason to marry is the instinctive mutual attraction of the two sexes to form a stable companionship of the two persons, as a basis for mutual happiness and help amid the trials of life extending even to sickness and old age."

Comparing this text with Pius' statement, we can see that the pope has in reality provided us with a gloss, and a most important one, on this text. I think that from what has been said thus far we can conclude that Pius XI is here, in effect, speaking of

---

[48] Pius XI, Encyclical *Casti connubii*, no. 23, in *Acta Apostolicae Sedis* 22 (1930): 548.

[49] Ibid., no. 24. In the official English text of *Casti connubii* no reference to the *Roman Catechism* is given. The Latin text, however, refers to *Catechismus Romanus*, part II, chap. VIII, 13; AAS 22 (1930): 548.

what the 1983 Code will call the "good of the spouses", and that he identifies it as an end of marriage.

Pius XI clearly shows that this end consists in the endeavor of the spouses, rooted in their unique and exclusive love for one another, to help each other perfect themselves and grow in holiness. In short, a married person's path to the holiness God wants him to have has a name: his or her spouse.[50]

Conclusion: The Family and Society

My fundamental argument has been that the human race survives only in its children, and its children can flourish fully only in the family rooted in the marriage of one man and one woman. Only if this truth is recognized can a "civilization of love" be developed.

But today this understanding of the family is under attack. According to the champions of "free sex", of utilitarianism and individualism, of militant feminism and the "gay" revolution, the creation of a family is essentially a matter of choice. According to those advocating these ideas the "family" should be redefined so as to emphasize bonds formed, not so much by marriage and kinship as by personal choices and declared commitment.[51] In other words, "family" ought to be defined primarily in terms of the free choices made by the individuals who form them—and who are free to leave them whenever they are so disposed.

This is folly. As we have seen, the future of the human race passes through the family rooted in the marriage of one man and one woman. Children *need* both a mother and a father. Mothering does not present the difficulties that fathering does. As one writer notes, "simply stated, an adult female will be naturally transformed into a social mother when she bears a child, but there is no corresponding natural transformation for a male."[52]

[50] Ibid., no. 23.

[51] See, for instance, Carol Levine, "AIDS and Changing Concepts of the Family", *Milbank Quarterly* 68, Suppl. 1 (1990): 36–37.

[52] Peter Wilson, *Man: the Promising Primate: The Conditions of Human Evolution*, 2nd ed. (New Haven: Yale University Press, 1983), p. 71.

The father-involved family, as another author points out, "is a fragile cultural achievement that cannot be taken for granted".[53]

The essence of the matter can be put this way: In order for a male to be induced to undertake the responsibility of fathering, he needs, first of all, to give himself unreservedly to a particular woman, who in turn must receive him and, in receiving him, give herself to him. Both the man and the woman, if the father's role is to be properly fulfilled, must give themselves to each other unreservedly. They must, in other words, take upon themselves the responsibility of marriage, of fidelity to each other, of selfless service to their children, of building a "civilization of love". Consequently, as John W. Miller has so eloquently put it, when "a culture ceases to support, through its mores, symbols, models, laws, and rituals, the sanctity of the sexual bond between a man and his wife and a father's involvement with his own children, powerful natural forces will inevitably take over in favor of the mother-alone family; the fragility of the sexual bond (and the investment of fathers with children) will give way to the strength of the primary bond between mother and child." [54]

This enables us to formulate a fourteenth moral criterion for families today: (14) *society must support the sanctity of the marriage bond if men are to be fathers to their children.*

I can end this chapter as follows. A slogan voiced by champions of "free love", utilitarianism, and individualism is that "no unwanted child ought ever to be born." This is banal. Opposed to it is a truth rooted in the reality of human existence, namely, that "no person, including children, ought to be unwanted." The only way to develop a society in which all human persons, including unborn children, are indeed loved and wanted is to respect the beauty of a family rooted in the marriage of one man and one woman. Only by doing so can the "civilization of love" become a reality.

---

[53] John W. Miller, *Biblical Faith and Fathering: Why We Call God "Father"* (New York: Paulist Press, 1989), p. 5.

[54] Ibid., p. 19. The text is italicized in the original. See also George Gilder, *Men and Marriage* (Gretna, La.: Pelican, 1986).

2

Marriage and the Complementarity of Male and Female

The "Beatifying Beginning" of Human Existence

It is fitting to begin our investigation into marriage and the complementarity of male and female with the first two chapters of Genesis. It is fitting to do so because these chapters, which contain the stories of what Pope John Paul II has called the "beatifying beginning of human existence",[1] set forth precious truths about men and women of utmost importance to our topic.

The narrative found in the first chapter of Genesis, attributed to the Priestly tradition, declares: "God created man [*ha 'adam*] in his image; in the divine image he created him; male and female he created them. God blessed them, saying: 'Be fertile and multiply; fill the earth and subdue it. Have dominion over the fish of the sea, the birds of the air, and all the living things that move on the earth'" (Gen 1:27–28).

In the second chapter of Genesis, attributed to the Yahwist source, we find the following:

> The Lord God formed man [*ha 'adam*] out of the clay of the ground and blew into his nostrils the breath of life, and so man became a living being. . . . The Lord God said: "It is not good for the man [*ha 'adam*] to be alone. I will make a suitable partner for

---

[1] See *Man and Woman*, 14.3, p. 182. In this text Pope John Paul II is explicitly concerned with the account in Genesis 2, but the expression "beatifying beginning" can also be applied to the narrative in Genesis 1.

him. . . ." The Lord God cast a deep sleep on the man, and while he was asleep, he took out one of his ribs and closed up its place with flesh. The Lord God then built up into a woman [*isshah*] the rib that he had taken from the man [*ha 'adam*]. When he brought her to the man [*ha 'adam*], the man [*ha 'adam*] said: "This one, at last, is bone of my bones and flesh of my flesh; This one shall be called 'woman' [*isshah*], for out of 'her man' [*ish*] this one has been taken." That is why a man [*ish*] leaves his father and mother and clings to his wife [*isshah*], and the two of them become one body. The man [*ish*] and his wife [*isshah*] were both naked, yet they felt no shame (Gen 2:7, 18, 21–25).

In my opinion, three crucial truths about men and women, marriage, and the complementarity of the sexes are rooted in these texts: (1) that men and women are equally persons; (2) that God is the author of marriage, the one who gives to it its defining characteristics; and (3) that men and women are body-persons, not spirit-persons.

1. The personhood of man and woman. That both man and woman are equally persons is luminously expressed in Genesis 1, even though it does not use the term *person*. But the text makes it clear that human beings, male and female, are persons, for it affirms that "God created man [*ha 'adam*] in his image; in the divine image he created him, male and female he created them" (Gen 1:27). Note that the Hebrew word, *adam*, is not used here as a proper name for the first human male, as it was in later texts of Genesis, but rather as the generic term to designate man, a human being, whether male or female. Being created in the image of God, man—male and female—is a person, i.e., a being endowed with intellect and will, with the capacity to come to know the truth, to make free choices, and by so doing to be self-determining. Both the man and the woman are thus persons, the sort of beings toward whom "the only proper and adequate attitude", as Karol Wojtyla has said, "is love".[2] And to these human persons made in his image, to the woman as well as to the man, God gave dominion

---

[2] *Love and Responsibility*, p. 41.

over the earth and the non-human creatures inhabiting it, its waters, and its atmosphere.

The truth that woman, like man, is a person is expressed more poetically in Genesis 2. There the man, who is initially identified by the generic term for human being, *adam*, is created first. But it is "not good" for him to be alone. The other living creatures of the earth, however, are not equal to him; they are not worthy to be his companion, his partner. Thus the Lord God, after casting the man into a deep sleep, forms from his rib a woman so that there can be a creature noble enough to be his partner, to share life with him. And on awakening from his sleep the man delights in finding this partner, this "bone of his bones and the flesh of his flesh", and in his delight gives to her the name *isshah*, "woman", and to himself the name *ish*, "man". Both are obviously regarded, in this text, as equal in their dignity, one far surpassing that of the other living creatures God has made.

In addition, if we reflect on these Genesis passages in the light of revelation, we realize that God, who created man and woman, is a God who is love and who, in himself, "lives a mystery of personal loving communion" in a Trinity of persons. It thus follows that by creating man and woman in his own image, by making them *persons*, "God inscribed into the humanity of man and woman the vocation, and thus the capacity and responsibility of love and communion." [3]

---

[3] *Familiaris consortio*, no. 11. All men and women are called to love and communion. As the Holy Father notes later in this same passage, "Christian revelation recognizes two specific ways of realizing the vocation of the human person, in its entirety, to love: marriage and virginity or celibacy. Either one is in its own proper form an actuation of the most profound truth of man, of his being 'created in the image of God'."

Some men and women freely choose celibacy in order to give themselves more fully to the service of our Lord and his people. Others, who may earnestly long to marry, accept celibacy because for one or another reason it is not possible for them to marry. For such men and women the requirements of the truth—of God's reign—impose a "situational celibacy". On this see the observations of Edward Schillebeeckx, O.P., *Marriage: Human Reality and Saving Mystery* (New York: Sheed and Ward, 1965), p. 120; see also Roger Balducelli, O.S.F.S., "The Decision for Celibacy", *Theological Studies* 36 (1975): 219–42.

2. God is the author of marriage. A second major feature of these texts is that they are accounts not only of the origin of the human race, male and female, but also of the origin of marriage. They proclaim that God is the author of marriage, the one who gives to it its "defining characteristics".[4] Indeed, it is to both these passages of Genesis that Jesus later referred when, in responding to the Pharisees' question about divorce, and in replying that it was only because of the "hardness" of human hearts that Moses had permitted divorce; he insisted that divorce was not God's will, for "At the beginning of creation God made them male and female [Gen 1:27]; for this reason a man shall leave his father and mother and the two shall become as one [Gen 2:24]. They are no longer two but one flesh. Therefore, let no man separate what God has joined" (Mk 10:6–9).

What are these "defining characteristics" of marriage? A central one is that marriage is an intimate, personal union between one man and one woman in which they "become one body, one flesh". By giving themselves to one another in marriage, a man and a woman actualize their vocation to love and to enter into a communion of persons.

Here it is important to note that the text of Genesis 2 clearly indicates that the reality of marriage comes to be when a man and a woman "give" themselves to one another by an act of irrevocable personal choice. As we saw in Chapter One, Pope John Paul II brings this out beautifully in his commentary on Genesis 2:24:

> The formulation of Genesis 2:24 itself indicates not only that human
> beings, created as man and woman, have been created for unity,

---

[4] *Marriage: Human Reality and Saving Mystery*, p. 24: "To be created by God, or to be named by him, implied a commission to serve him. The whole of the Old Testament ethic of marriage and family was based on this. The things of the earth and man received their *hoq* or *huqqah* [their statutes of limitation, their defining characteristics] with their creation; each received, on creation, its intrinsic conditions of existence, its defined limits." That God is the author of marriage has always been affirmed by the Magisterium of the Church. See, for example, Council of Trent, DS, no. 1797; *Casti connubii*, DS, no. 3700; *Gaudium et spes*, no. 48.

but also that precisely this *unity, through which they become "one flesh," has from the beginning the character of a union that derives from a choice.* We read, in fact, "a man will leave his father and his mother and unite with his wife." While the man, by virtue of generation, belongs "by nature" to his father and mother, "he unites," by contrast, with his wife (or she with her husband) by choice. The text of Genesis 2:24 defines this character of the conjugal bond in reference to the first man and the first woman, but at the same time it does so also in the perspective of man's earthly future as a whole. In his own time, therefore, Christ was to appeal to this text as equally relevant in his age. Since they are formed in the image of God also inasmuch as they form an authentic communion of persons, the first man and the first woman must constitute the beginning and model of that for all men and women who in any period unite with each other so intimately that they are "one flesh." The body, which through its own masculinity and femininity helps the two ("a help similar to himself") from the beginning to find themselves in a communion of persons [see *Gaudium et Spes*, 24.3], becomes in a particular way the constitutive element of their union when they become husband and wife. This takes place, however, through a reciprocal choice. The choice is what establishes the conjugal covenant between the persons, who become "one flesh" only based on this choice. (*Man and Woman* 10.3, p. 168)

The act of marital consent is an act of choice, whereby the man chooses this particular woman as the irreplaceable and non-substitutable person with whom he wills to share his life henceforward until death, and whereby the woman in turn chooses this particular man as the irreplaceable and nonsubstitutable person with whom she wills to share her life henceforward until death. Marriage is, therefore, the intimate partnership of life and love between man and woman, brought into being by their own act of irrevocable personal consent.

Another "defining characteristic" of marriage is set forth in Genesis 1, where the man and the woman—the husband and wife—are blessed and commanded to "be fertile and multiply" (Gen 1:28). This text shows that marriage and the intimate partnership of love and life that it establishes between man and woman is ordered to the procreation and education of children.[5] Inasmuch as the union of man and woman in marriage is dynamically oriented to the generation of new human life, we can see one of the reasons why God created man in two differing but complementary sexes, male and female. The human race is sexually differentiated into male and female because it must be so if it is to survive. A man cannot generate new human life with another man, nor can a woman do so with another woman. In generating human life man and woman do indeed "complement" one another. Fertility, we need to keep in mind, is a blessing from God, and it requires the complementary fertility of husband and wife. One biblical scholar, commenting on this passage, has appropriately observed that "Progeny is a gift from God, the fruit of his blessing. Progeny are conceived because of the divine power which has been transferred to men." And, he continues, "[T]he blessing ... indicates that fertility is the purpose of the sexual distinction, albeit not the exclusive purpose of this distinction."[6]

3. Men and women are body-persons, not spirit persons. A third critically important feature of these texts is that they characterize human persons, male and female, as bodily beings. As Leon Kass has noted,

> The account in Genesis 1 describes them as living beings who are bodily and sexual in nature, blessed with fertility and summoned to multiply their kind. Genesis 2 is even more graphic in showing the bodily character of the human beings whom God, as Genesis 1 instructs us, created in his own image. For Genesis 2 shows that man is constituted by two principles, one low ("dust of the earth"),

[5] On this see *Gaudium et spes*, no. 48: "By its very nature the institution of marriage and married love is ordered to the procreation and education of the offspring and it is in them that it finds its crowning glory." See also no. 50: "Marriage and married love are by nature ordered to the procreation and education of children. Indeed, children are the supreme gift of marriage and greatly contribute to the good of the parents themselves."

[6] Raymond Collins, "The Bible and Sexuality I", *Biblical Theology Bulletin* 7 (1977): 156.

one high ("breath of life"). The human being first comes to sight as a formed and animated (or breathing) dust of the ground. Higher than the earth, yet still bound to it, the human being has a name, *adam* (from *adamah*, meaning "earth" or "ground"), which reminds him of his lowly terrestrial origins. Man is, from the start, up from below and in between.[7]

Moreover, it is clear from Genesis 2 that the human body is personal in nature and that it reveals or discloses the person. For "the man", on awakening from the deep sleep into which the Lord God had cast him and on seeing "the woman" who had been formed from his rib, declares: "she is flesh from my flesh and bone from my bones" (Gen 2:23). Commenting on this John Paul II declares that in uttering this cry, the man "seems to say, *Look, a body that expresses the 'person'!*" (*Man and Woman*, 14.4, p. 183). Men and women, in other words, are persons, but they are not spirits or disembodied minds. When God created man he did not, as some dualistic-minded theologians today think, create "an isolated subjectivity ... who experiences existence in [either] a female body-structure ... [or] a male body-structure".[8] Quite to the contrary, God, in creating *human* persons, created persons who are bodily in nature.

This is a matter of utmost importance. Human persons are bodily, sexual beings. Their sexuality, "by means of which man and woman give themselves to one another through the acts mutual and exclusive to spouses, is by no means something merely biological, but concerns the innermost being of the human person as such",[9] and it does so because human sexuality is the sexuality of a human

[7] Leon Kass, "Man and Woman: An Old Story", *First Things: A Monthly Journal of Religion and Public Life* 17 (November 1991): 16.

[8] On this see Anthony Kosnik et al., *Human Sexuality: New Directions in American Catholic Thought: A Study Commissioned by the Catholic Theological Society of America* (New York: Paulist, 1977), pp. 83–84, hereafter cited as Kosnik, *Human Sexuality*. An excellent critique of the dualism underlying much contemporary thought, including that of influential Catholic theologians, is provided by Germain Grisez, "Dualism and the New Morality", in *Atti del Congresso Internazionale (Roma-Napoli, 17–24 Aprile 1974): Tommaso d'Aquino nel suo Settimo Centenario*, vol. 5, *L'Agire Morale* (Naples: Edizioni Domenicane Napoli, 1977).

[9] *Familiaris consortio*, no. 11.

person and is hence personal in character. Sexuality has to do with our bodiliness. Our bodies, however, are not impersonal instruments that are to be used *by* our persons; instead, they are integral components of our *being* as *persons*. From this it follows that the more apparent anatomical differences between males and females are, as one contemporary writer puts it, "not mere accidentals or mere attachments ... [instead], differences in the body are *revelations* of differences in the depths of their being." [10]

The human body, in other words, is a revelation of a human person; and since the human body is inescapably either male or female, it is the revelation of a man-person or a woman-person. Precisely because of their sexual differences, manifest in their bodies, the man-person and the woman-person can give themselves to one another bodily. Moreover, since the body, male or female, is the expression of a human person, a man and a woman, in giving their bodies to one another, give their *persons* to one another. The bodily gift of a man and a woman to each other is the outward sign, the sacrament, of the *communion of persons* existing between them. And this sacrament, in turn, is an image of the communion of persons in the Trinity. The body, therefore, is the means and the sign of the gift of the man-person to the woman-person. Pope John Paul II calls this capacity of the body to express the communion of persons the *spousal meaning* (see *Man and Woman*, 14–16). [11] It is precisely for this reason that genital coition outside of marriage is gravely immoral. When unmarried individuals have sex, the sex act does not unite two irreplaceable and nonsubstitutable persons but rather joins two individuals who are in principle disposable, replaceable, and substitutable. But when husband and wife give themselves to one another in the marital act, they do so as irreplaceable and

---

[10] Robert E. Joyce, in Mary Rosera Joyce and Robert E. Joyce, *New Dynamics in Sexual Love* (Collegeville, Minn.: St. John's University Press, 1970), pp. 34–35.

[11] The translation *spousal* meaning is that used by Waldstein; earlier translations used the term *nuptial* in place of *spousal*. On the "spousal" or "nuptial" meaning of the body in John Paul II's Theology of the Body see Christopher West, *The Theology of the Body Explained: A Commentary on John Paul II's "Gospel of the Body"* (rev. ed.: Boston: Pauline Books and Media, 2007).

nonsubstitutable spouses. Pope John Paul II has expressed this truth eloquently:

> The total physical self-giving would be a lie if it were not the sign and fruit of a total personal self-giving, in which the whole person, including the temporal dimension, is present.... The only "place" in which this self-giving in its whole truth is made possible is marriage, the covenant of conjugal love freely and consciously chosen, whereby man and woman accept the intimate community of life and love willed by God himself, which only in this light manifests its true meaning.[12]

Our examination of the Genesis texts has shown us that man and woman are equally persons, that God has made them for each other, and that they are complementary in their sexuality. But the nature of their sexual complementarity needs to be set forth in more detail. It is evident that their sexual complementarity is intimately related to their vocation to marriage and parenthood. Indeed, as the *Catechism of the Catholic Church* teaches, "everyone, man and woman, should acknowledge and accept his sexual *identity*. Physical, moral, and spiritual *difference* and *complementarity* are oriented toward the goods of marriage and the flourishing of family life."[13] Husbands and wives, as we have seen in examining the "defining characteristics" of marriage, have the high vocation, the *munus* or noble responsibility, to cooperate with God in handing on human life and in giving to new human life the home where it can take root and grow.[14] Not all men and women, of course, become husbands and wives, fathers and mothers. Yet all men are potentially fathers and all women are potentially mothers. Even if they do not generate children, as men and women they are called upon to exercise analogously a kind of spiritual

[12] *Familiaris consortio*, no. 11.

[13] CCC 2333.

[14] A rich analysis of the Latin term *munus*, used in many magisterial texts to designate the vocation to parenthood, is provided by Janet Smith. See her *Humanae Vitae: A Generation Later* (Washington, D.C.: Catholic University of America, 1991), esp. pp. 136–48. See also her "The *Munus* of Transmitting Human Life: A New Approach to *Humanae Vitae*", *Thomist* 54 (1990): 385–427.

fatherhood and spiritual motherhood in the living out of their lives.

I will now endeavor to express more specifically the complementarity of male and female. I will begin by reflecting on the act which is "proper and exclusive to spouses",[15] namely the marital act.

The Marital Act as Expressing and Symbolizing the Complementarity of Male and Female

A man and a woman become husband and wife when they give themselves to each other in and through the act of irrevocable personal consent that makes them to *be* spouses. They become literally "one flesh", "one body", when they consummate their marriage and give themselves to each other in the act proper and exclusive to them as spouses, the spousal or the marital act. In this act they come intimately to "know"[16] each other in an unforgettable way, and to know each other precisely as male and female.

The marital act is a unique kind of act. It is the personal act of two subjects, husband and wife. In it they "give" themselves to one another and "receive" one another. Yet they do so in strikingly different and complementary ways, for it is an act made possible precisely by reason of their sexual differences. The wife does not have a penis; therefore, in this act of marital union she cannot enter the body, the person, of her husband, whereas he can and does personally enter into her body-person. He gives himself to her and by doing so he receives her. On the other hand, she is uniquely capable of receiving her husband personally into her body, her self, and in so doing she gives herself to him. The wife's receiving of her husband in a giving sort of way is just as essential to the unique meaning of this act as is her husband's giving of himself to her in a receiving sort of way. The husband cannot, in this act, give himself to his wife unless she gives herself

---

[15] *Familiaris consortio*, no. 11.

[16] "Adam *knew* Eve his wife, and she conceived and bore Cain, saying: 'I have begotten a man with the help of the Lord'" (Gen 4:1, emphasis added).

to him by receiving him, nor can she receive him in this self-giving way unless he gives himself to her in this receiving way.[17] As the philosopher Robert Joyce says, "the man does not force himself upon the woman, but gives himself in a receiving manner. The woman does not simply submit herself to the man, but receives him in a giving manner."[18] Note that in the marital act the husband is not active and the wife passive. Each is active, but is active in differing and complementary ways.

In giving himself to his wife in the marital act, moreover, the husband releases into her body-person millions of his sperm which go in search for an ovum. Should his wife indeed be fertile and an ovum present within her fallopian tubes, one of the sperm may succeed in uniting with it, in becoming "one flesh" with it, and in doing so bring into existence a new human person. These facts dramatically illumine another dimension or aspect of the male-female sexual complementarity. The man, as it were, symbolizes the superabundance and differentiation of being, for his sperm are differentiated into those that will generate a male child and those that will generate a female child. The woman, as it were, symbolizes the oneness or unity of being (insofar as she ordinarily releases only one ovum) and what we might call the withinness or abidingness of being.[19]

[17] When nonmarried males and females engage in sexual coition, they do not "give" themselves to each other or "receive" each other. Their act in no way expresses and symbolizes personal union precisely because they have refused to give and receive each other unconditionally as persons. In genital union, such individuals do not make a "gift" of themselves to each other; rather, they use each other as means to attain subjectively determined ends.

[18] Robert E. Joyce, *Human Sexual Ecology: A Philosophy and Ethics of Man and Woman* (Washington, D.C.: University Press of America, 1980), pp. 70–71.

[19] On this see Joyce, ibid., pp. 70–71: "The man emphasizes in his way the giving power of being and the *otherness* of every being in the universe.... The man emphasizes (with his sperm production) manyness, differentiation, and plurality ... characteristics based on uniqueness and otherness." The woman, on the other hand, "emphasizes ... the receiving power of her being and the *withinness* of every being in the universe.... The woman emphasizes (with her ova production) oneness and sameness ... characteristics based on withinness and superrelatedness."

In reflecting on the significance of the marital act we can also say, I believe, that the man, the husband, is the one who emphasizes, in giving himself wholeheartedly to his wife, an outgoing, productive kind of joyful existence, while the woman, the wife, is the one who emphasizes, in receiving her husband wholeheartedly into her person, the abidingness and peaceful tranquility of existence.

"Defining" Man and Woman, Male and Female

What this analysis of the marital act suggests is that human sexuality is a giving and a receiving, a superabundant, outgoing otherness and a peaceful, rest-bringing withinness. By virtue of their sexuality—which, we must remember, is not something merely biological but something that "concerns the innermost being of the human person"—men and women are summoned to give themselves to others and to receive them, and to do so in a unique and exclusive way in marriage. They are likewise summoned to be outgoing and superabundant in their giving and to bring others peace and rest by receiving them within themselves. But men and women, males and females, give superabundantly and receive in peaceful tranquility in strikingly different modalities.

Human sexuality, in other words, is realized differently in male and female, in man and woman. Male sexuality emphasizes giving in a receiving sort of way and the superabundant plenitude and otherness of being; female sexuality emphasizes receiving in a giving sort of way and the peace-giving, rest-bringing withinness of being. It therefore seems to me that Joyce's way of "defining" man and woman is correct. He does so as follows:

> I would define a man as a human being who both gives in a receiving way and receives in a giving way, but is so structured in his being that he is emphatically inclined toward giving in a receiving way. The nature of being a man is an emphasis on giving in a receiving way. A woman is a human being who both gives in a receiving way and receives in a giving way, but is so structured in her being that she is emphatically inclined toward receiving in a

giving way. The nature of being a woman is an emphasis on receiving in a giving way. . . . The sexuality of man and woman . . . is orientated in opposite but very complementary ways.[20]

Here it is most important to note that, in a very profound passage in which he reflects on the way men and women "give" and "receive" each other, John Paul II declared:

> While in the mystery of creation the woman is the one who is "given" to the man, he on his part, in receiving her as a gift in the full truth of her person and femininity, enriches her by this very reception, and, at the same time, he too is enriched in this reciprocal relationship. The man is enriched not only through her, who gives her own person and femininity to him, but also by his gift of self. The man's act of self-donation, in answer to that of the woman, is for him himself an enrichment; in fact, it is here that *the specific essence, as it were, of his masculinity is manifested, which, through the reality of the body and of its sex, reaches the innermost depth of "self-possession,"* thanks to which he is able both to give himself and to receive the gift of the other. The man, therefore, not only accepts the gift, but at the same time is welcomed as a gift by the woman in the self-revelation of the inner spiritual essence of his masculinity together with the whole truth of his body and his sex. . . . It follows that such an acceptance, in which the man finds himself through the "sincere gift of self," becomes in him a source of a new and more profound enrichment of the woman with himself. The exchange is reciprocal, and the mutual effects of the "sincere gift" and of "finding oneself" reveal themselves and grow in that exchange [*Gaudium et Spes*, 24.3]. (*Man and Woman*, 17.6, p. 197)

I emphasized the passage in which the pope says that the specific essence of man's masculinity enables him to give himself and to receive the other's gift. I do so because I believe that this passage shows that the view taken by Robert Joyce and accepted by me that sex involves both a giving and a receiving, and that man and woman are called both to give and to receive, but that the man is the one who emphatically *gives in a receiving way*, whereas the

[20] Ibid., pp. 67–69.

woman is the one who emphatically *receives in a giving way*, harmonizes well with John Paul II's Theology of the Body.

Moreover, as we have seen, the man emphasizes in his being the superabundant otherness or plenitude of being whereas the woman emphasizes its withinness and abidingness, its capacity to bring rest and peace. Man and woman, we must remember, are made in the image of God. They are two differing and complementary ways of imaging him. He is both the superabundant giver of good gifts and the One who is ever within us, who is with us and for us, and who longs to welcome us and to give our hearts refreshment and peace. He is, as the beautiful hymn of Henry Van Dyck expresses it, both the "Wellspring of the joy of living" and the "Ocean depth of happy rest".[21] Both man and woman are to image God in his superabundant goodness and his peaceful immanence, to image him as the "Wellspring of the joy of living" and "Ocean depth of happy rest". But the man, in imaging God, emphasizes his transcendent, superabundant goodness, his glory as the "Wellspring of the joy of living", while the woman, in imaging God, emphasizes his immanence, his "withinness", his glory as the "Ocean depth of happy rest".

The man, like the woman, is summoned to receive as well as to give, to be an "ocean depth of happy rest" as well as a "wellspring of the joy of living"; the woman, like the man, is summoned to give as well as to receive, to be a "wellspring of the joy of living" as well as an "ocean depth of happy rest". Since this is so, it is reasonable to hold that within every human person, male or female, there is the "masculine" (the emphasis on giving in a receiving way, on being a "wellspring of the joy of living") and the "feminine" (the emphasis on receiving in a giving way, on being an "ocean depth of happy rest").[22] It is therefore possible

[21] Henry Van Dyck, "Joyful, Joyful, We Adore Thee", *Poems of Henry Van Dyck* (New York: Charles Scribner's Sons, n.d.). This beautiful hymn has been set to music, using as the musical score a chorus from Beethoven's Ninth Symphony.

[22] Joyce, *Human Sexual Ecology*, p. 68, expresses this idea by saying that his way of defining man and woman "takes into account that every person is male [I would say 'masculine' rather than 'male'] or female [I would say 'feminine' rather than 'female'] within. Every person has a human nature, which includes the ability

to think of a man as a being who dynamically combines maleness, the masculine, and the feminine, while the woman is one who dynamically combines femaleness, the feminine, and the masculine. This in no way, however, as Prudence Allen among others has noted, implies that we are moving "to an androgyny, or a theory of identity of all human beings, because the starting point, the maleness or femaleness, is always different for the two sexes. The combination of the three factors of male, masculine, and feminine in a male individual would always differ from the combination of the three factors of female, masculine, and feminine in a female individual." [23] The point is that males and females, men and women, embrace within themselves the masculine and the feminine, but they embody and manifest these aspects of their personality in differing and complementary ways.

Precisely because the woman's sexuality emphasizes the withinness, the abidingness, the sameness of being and because the man's sexuality emphasizes the outgoingness, the expansiveness, the otherness of being, a woman's sexual identity is more interior, intimately linked to her being, her bodiliness, whereas a man's sexual identity is more exterior, intimately associated with his activity. It is for this reason, as numerous studies have shown,[24] that a woman

---

and the tendency to share the gift of self. Both a man and a woman are structured in a way that naturally enables them to give in a receiving sort of way and to receive in a giving sort of way.... But the nature of man is a dynamic orientation to emphasize, at all levels of his being, the receiving kind of giving, while the nature of a woman is a dynamic orientation to emphasize, at all levels of her being, the giving kind of receiving."

[23] Sister Prudence Allen, "Integral Sexual Complementarity and the Theology of Communion", *Communio: International Catholic Review* 17 (1990): 533.

[24] See for example, the following: J. Bardwick, *Psychology of Women* (New York: Harper and Row, 1971); Margaret Mead, *Male and Female* (New York: Dell, 1949); Robert Stoller, M.D., *Sex and Gender: On the Development of Masculinity and Femininity* (New York: Science House, 1968); Lionel Tiger, *Men in Groups* (New York: Random House, 1969). Their common point is that men need to go out of themselves in order to discover and secure their masculinity whereas women do not. An interesting account of this issue is provided by Walter Ong, S.J., *Fighting for Life: Contest, Sexuality, and Consciousness* (Ithaca: Cornell University Press, 1981), esp. pp. 70–80, 97–98, 112–15. This accounts for the fact, as Ong notes, "[T]he

more easily comes to a realization of what it means to be feminine and a woman than a man does in coming to realize what it means to be masculine and a man. The man needs, as it were, to go out of himself and prove himself in the world.

Insofar as they differ in their sexuality, men and women manifest major differences in their social behavior. Women, as many studies point out, tend toward responding to situations as entire persons, with their minds, bodies, and emotions integrated, whereas men tend to respond in a more diffuse and differentiated manner. Again, women are, on the whole, more oriented toward helping or caring for personal needs, whereas men, on the whole, are more inclined to formulate and pursue long-range goals and to achieve particular sets of prescribed ends.[25] Or, to put the matter somewhat differently, we might say, with Steven Clark, that "in social situations men are more oriented to goals outside the situation (what the situation can become), women to internal goals (relieving needs, giving comfort and pleasure)."[26] Note, however, that all this is a matter of *emphasis*, corresponding to the ways in which men and women tend to emphasize their sexuality. Men, too, can and do respond as entire persons and care for personal needs, and women, too, can and do differentiate between their emotions and their intelligent judgments and make long-range plans. But the tendencies noted are real and correspond to the personalities of men and women as sexual persons.

---

received symbol for woman, Venus's mirror (♀), adopted by feminists apparently everywhere, signifies self-possession, gazing at oneself as projected into the outside world or environment and reflected back into the self from there, whole. The received symbol for man, Mars's spear (♂), signifies conflict, change, stress, dissection, division" (p. 77).

[25] On this see Steven Clark, *Man and Woman in Christ: An Examination of the Roles of Men and Women in Light of Scripture and the Social Sciences* (Ann Arbor, Mich.: Servant Books, 1980). In chapters sixteen and seventeen (pp. 371–466) Clark summarizes relevant material from the descriptive social sciences and experimental psychology bearing on the differences between males and females. Clark supplies an exhaustive search of the literature, providing excellent bibliographical notes.

[26] Ibid., p. 390.

With this understanding of man and woman, male and female, and of their sexual complementarity in mind, we can now look more closely at the relationship between man and woman in marriage and to their vocation as fathers and mothers.

Woman as Mother, Man as Father

The marital act, which expresses and symbolizes the complementary sexuality of man and woman, is an act that is open not only to the communication of a unique and exclusive love proper to husbands and wives but also to the communication of life. For it is in and through the marital act that new human life comes to be in the way God wills that it come to be. New human life can, of course, come to be in and through the acts of adulterers and fornicators, and when it comes to be in this way, the new human life is indeed a new human person, a being to be loved and cherished and respected by all. But when new human life comes to be in this way, it is insulted and harmed, and a tragedy has occurred. For nonmarried men and women do not have the right to generate new human life, just as they do not have the right to engage in coition. They do not have the right to generate human life precisely because they have not, through their own free choice to marry one another, given to themselves the capacity to receive life lovingly, to nourish it humanely, and to educate it in the love and service of God and neighbor.[27]

God wills that new human life come to be in and through the loving marital act of husbands and wives. He does so because they have, precisely by virtue of the fact that they have given themselves unconditionally and unreservedly to one another in marriage, capacitated themselves to receive human life lovingly, nourish it humanely, and educate it in the love and service of God and neighbor. They are the ones who can give this new life the home that it needs to take root and grow.

When new human life comes to be in and through the marital act, it comes to be *within* the wife, within the mother. This new

---

[27] St. Augustine, *De genesi ad literam*, 9, 7 (PL 34:1397).

life, like every human life, is, as Pope John Paul II says, entrusted "to each and every other human being, but in a special way the human being is entrusted to woman, precisely because the woman in virtue of her special experience of motherhood is seen to have *a specific sensitivity* towards the human person and all that constitutes the individual's true welfare, beginning with the fundamental value of life".[28] Indeed, as the late Holy Father also observes,

> Motherhood involves a special communion with the mystery of life as it develops in the woman's womb. The mother is filled with wonder at this mystery of life and "understands" with unique intuition what is happening inside her. In the light of the "beginning," the mother accepts and loves as a person the child she is carrying in her womb. This unique contact with the new human being developing within her gives rise to an attitude toward human beings—not only towards her own child, but every human being—which profoundly marks the woman's personality. It is commonly thought that women are more capable than men of paying attention to another person and that motherhood develops this predisposition even more. The man—even with all his sharing in parenthood—always remains "outside" the process of pregnancy and the baby's birth; in many ways he has to *learn* his own *"fatherhood" from the mother.* . . . [T]he mother's contribution is decisive in laying the foundation for a new human personality.[29]

We can see here how, in motherhood, the woman's sexuality as a "receiving in a giving sort of way" and as symbolizing the withinness of being and God as the "ocean depth of happy rest" is manifested. Moreover, as the remarks of John Paul II indicate, the tendency of women to respond integrally to situations, with mind, body, and emotions integrated, and to be oriented to personal needs is magnificently revealed in motherhood. In his

[28] Pope John Paul II, apostolic exhortation *Christifideles Laici*, no. 51. See also apostolic letter *Mulieris Dignitatem*, no. 30: "The moral and spiritual strength of a woman is joined to her awareness that *God entrusts the human being to her in a special way.* Of course, God entrusts every human being to each and every other human being. But this entrusting concerns women in a special way—precisely because of their femininity—and this in a particular way determines their vocation."

[29] *Mulieris Dignitatem*, no. 18.

comments, he referred to the woman's "unique intuition" and "understanding" of what is going on within her. Here what he has to say fits in well with what we have seen before about the psychic-spiritual life of women, and indeed seems to be corroborated by all that we know about their lives. I believe that Benedict Ashley has summarized this matter well. He writes:

> From such empirical studies as are available, the common saying that women are more "intuitive" than men is probably correct. Human intelligence, as St. Thomas Aquinas pointed out, has two phases. The first phase is *intellectus, ratio superior*, "insight," or "intuition" by which we grasp certain seminal truths directly from our sense experience with a certainty based immediately on that experience. The second phase is *ratio, ratio inferior*, "reason," by which we explicitate and develop these seminal truths by a logical calculus.... It is not strange that women on the average rely more on insight, men on reason. While this can be attributed to the support given by our culture to these different modes of thought, yet they are perhaps more deeply and genetically rooted in the fact that women in order to succeed in their ... role as mothers have needed a more penetrating intuition than do men in order to deal effectively with personal relations so needed in the family.[30]

The woman, therefore, is the one to whom new human life is entrusted in a very special way. But she is, precisely because of her sexuality and her way of imaging God, prepared to receive it lovingly and give it the care it needs in order to take root and grow.

It is important to stress here the immense contribution that mothers make to human civilization in carrying out responsibly their vocation to receive new human life and to care generously for it, especially during its early years. While women indeed have,

[30] Benedict Ashley, O.P., "Moral Theology and Mariology", *Anthropotes: Rivista di Studi sulla Persona e la Famiglia* 7.2 (December 1991): 147. Ashley refers to Mary F. Belensky et al., *Women's Ways of Knowing: The Development of Self, Voice, and Mind* (New York: Basic Books, 1988) for an empirical study supporting the idea that women are more intuitive than men. He refers to St. Thomas Aquinas, *Summa theologiae* I, q. 79, a. 9; *2 Sent.*, d. 24, q. 2, a. 2; and *De Veritate*, q. 15, a. 2 for the distinction between *intellectus, ratio superior* and *ratio, ratio inferior*.

as Pope John Paul II has emphasized, "the same right as men to perform various public services", it nonetheless remains true, as he has likewise said, that "society must be structured in such a way that wives and mothers are not in practice compelled to work outside the home." And it is absolutely imperative to overcome "the mentality which honors women more for their work outside the home than for their work within the family".[31]

But new human life is also entrusted to the man, to the husband. He is its father. But fathering, as indicated by Pope John Paul II in one of the passages cited above, is something that man must learn. Mothering, too, entails learning. But it is universally recognized that fatherhood and, in particular, the fatherhood necessary for a father-involved family, is much more a cultural achievement than is mothering. As Peter Wilson has put it, "simply stated, an adult female will be naturally transformed into a social mother when she bears a child, but there is no corresponding natural transformation for a male."[32]

In order for children, boys and girls, to develop well as integral persons, they need their fathers' care. Their fathers must become involved in their families.[33] The bond between children and their mother is strong by virtue of their symbiotic tie during pregnancy, birth, and nursing. Indeed, as John W. Miller has said, "it is this biologically determined relationship, so essential in laying the foundations of healthy development, that shapes those qualities usually associated with mothering: unconditional availability, receptivity, and tenderness."[34] But for the well-being of these children the fathers' loving presence is needed. When they are effectively present to their families and to their children, fathers must, as Miller notes, "insert themselves into the bond between mother and child as a 'second other' by an initiative very much

---

[31] *Familiaris consortio*, no. 23.

[32] Peter Wilson, *Man the Promising Primate: The Condition of Human Evolution*, 2nd ed. (New Haven: Yale University Press, 1983), p. 71; cited by John W. Miller, *Biblical Faith and Fathering: Why We Call God "Father"* (New York: Paulist, 1989), p. 11.

[33] See Introduction to Second edition, pp. ix–xiv above.

[34] Miller, *Biblical Faith and Fathering*, p. 57.

like that of adoption. Where this initiative is energetic and winsome," he continues:

> an essential autonomy from the mother is fostered and children of
> both sexes are significantly helped in orienting themselves to the
> cultural universe outside the home. . . . Maternal values are not thereby
> repudiated—fathers too may embody tender mother-like attributes
> without ceasing to be fathers—but the exclusivity of the mother-
> bond is challenged by an authority that separates the child and ori-
> ents it toward its personal future in extra-familial society.[35]

But for fathers to succeed in this task, they must properly manifest their sexual complementarity to their wives and the mothers
of their children. From all that has been said thus far, we can see
that for fathers to do this they must be seen as those who emphatically give in a receiving sort of way, who image God as the wellspring of the joy of living. We have already seen that, on the
whole, men tend to be more differentiated in their responses to
persons and situations, to be more goal-oriented; their sexual identity depends to a much greater extent than does a woman's on
what they do. While a woman nurtures, a man, as Ashley puts it,
"tends to *construct*, i.e., to impose an order on things, whether it
is the simple physical fact of initiating pregnancy, providing the
home as shelter and protection, or the more spiritual tasks of
disciplining the children physically and mentally, or undertaking
the work of the wider social order. Where the woman *allows* the
child to grow, the father *causes* the child to grow." [36]

The father has the primary responsibility to provide his wife
and his children with food, shelter, and protection, particularly
during her pregnancy and their infancy, to give his children (and
their mother) a sense of security by his presence and reliability. In
saying that the father has the responsibility to provide for his wife
and children, I do not mean to foreclose the possibility that in
specific families the wife-mother may be the one who contributes more economically to the family. It may be that she has
special talents and has acquired more marketably profitable capacities

[35] Ibid.
[36] Ashley, "Moral Theology and Mariology", 140.

and could therefore more adequately meet the financial needs of the family than could the husband-father. But even in such situations, it is nonetheless still the husband-father's primary responsibility to see to it that the wife and children are provided for. Only if he is allowed to do so can he dynamically combine his maleness with the masculine and the feminine within him.

The father-involved family is a fragile cultural achievement. And a family will be father-involved only if the husband-father is given the support necessary to be the one who gives in a receiving sort of way, who is the wellspring of the joy of living. If a culture ceases to support and encourage "through its mores, symbols, models, laws, and rituals, the sanctity of the bond between a man and his wife and a father's involvement with his own children, powerful natural forces will inevitably take over in favor of the mother-alone family." [37] And this is a tragedy.

Here it is important to realize that fathering and mothering are by no means mutually exclusive. The complementarity between males and females is sharply differentiated at their biological roots—only the woman can conceive and nurture the child within her womb and nurse it after birth. Nonetheless, the personality and character traits (the "masculine" and the "feminine", the "wellspring of the joy of living" and the "ocean depth of happy rest") are present in both males and females, although, as we have seen, with different emphases in each. Children need to be both accepted and nurtured, to be challenged and held to standards, and both mothers and fathers must accept and nurture their children, challenge them and hold them to standards. But they do so in somewhat differing modalities, with the mothers accentuating acceptance and nurturance, the fathers challenging and disciplining.[38]

---

[37] Miller, *Biblical Faith and Fathering*, p. 19.

[38] Worthwhile observations concerning the indispensable help fathers can give their children by communicating to them the knowledge and techniques they need to deal with the wider world, by setting standards and challenging them, are provided by Basil Cole, O.P., "Reflexions pour une spiritualite masculine", trans. Guy Beduelle, O.P., *Sources* (Fribourg) 12 (March–April 1987): 49–55. See also James B. Stenson, *Successful Fathers*, Scepter Booklet No. 181/182 (Princeton, N.J.: Scepter, 1989).

Before concluding these reflections on marriage and male-female complementarity, it is necessary to examine, albeit much too briefly here, the significance of the third chapter of Genesis and of the fifth chapter of Ephesians relative to marriage and the complementarity of male and female.

Genesis 3:16 and Ephesians 5:21–33

The third chapter of Genesis tells the story of the disobedience of man and woman (Adam and Eve) to God and their "fall". It shows how their sin terribly harmed human persons and, in particular, the male-female relationship in marriage. In punishing the woman for her disobedience God said, "[Y]our desire shall be for your husband, and he shall be your master" (Gen 3:16). As a result of the fall, concupiscence entered the human heart. Because of their physical strength and because the biology of the generative process allows men more opportunities to abuse their role, husbands and fathers, unfortunately, have often led the way in irresponsibility. Mothers and wives have, on the other hand, been tempted to become manipulative.[39] A "re-creation" of human persons, male and female, and of marriage itself was needed.

This "re-creation", thanks to God's bounteous mercy and goodness, has indeed taken place. For he has sent us his Son to redeem us and to bring us to a new kind of life. Through the saving death and resurrection of Jesus we have been liberated from sin and made new creatures. Through baptism we die to the "old man", to Adamic man, to sinful man, and put on the new man, Christ.

The marriage of Christians, of those who have, through baptism, become one with Christ and members of his body, is moreover a sacrament. It is a holy sign of the life-giving, love-giving union between Christ and his bride the Church. And not only is it a holy sign of this life-giving, love-giving union, but it is also,

---

[39] On this see the perceptive comments of Mary Stewart van Leeuwen, *Gender and Grace* (Westmont, Ill.: InterVarsity Press, 1990), pp. 44–48.

for those men and women who clothe themselves with Christ and abide in his love, an *effective* sign of this union, one that they can, with God's grace, realize in their own married lives and in this way mediate to the world the redemptive love of Christ. As Pope John Paul II said,

> The Spirit which the Lord pours forth gives a new heart, and renders man and woman capable of loving one another as Christ has loved us. Conjugal love reaches that fullness to which it is interiorly ordained, conjugal charity, which is the proper and specific way in which the spouses participate in and are called to live the very charity of Christ, who gave himself on the cross.... [B]y means of baptism, man and woman are definitively placed within the new and eternal covenant, in the spousal covenant of Christ with the Church. And it is because of this indestructible insertion that the intimate community of conjugal life and love, founded by the Creator, is elevated and assumed into the spousal charity of Christ, sustained and enriched by his redeeming power.[40]

Because of this Pope John Paul II continued, "Spouses are ... the permanent reminder to the Church of what happened on the Cross; they are for one another and for their children witnesses to the salvation in which the sacrament makes them sharers."[41]

The beauty of Christian marriage as an image of the bridal relationship between Christ and his Church is set forth eloquently in the Epistle to the Ephesians, where we read:

> Defer to one another out of reverence for Christ. Wives should be submissive to their husbands, as if to the Lord, because the husband is the head of his wife just as Christ is head of his body the church, as well as its savior. As the church submits to Christ, so wives should submit to their husbands in everything. Husbands, love your wives, as Christ loved the church. He gave himself up for her to make her holy, purifying her in the bath of water by the power of the word, to present to himself a glorious church, holy and immaculate, without stain or wrinkle or anything of that sort. Husbands should love their wives as they do

---

[40] *Familiaris consortio*, no. 13.
[41] Ibid.

their own bodies. He who loves his wife loves himself. Observe that no one ever hates his own flesh; no, he nourishes it and takes care of it as Christ cares for the church—for we are members of his body. For this reason a man shall leave his father and mother, and shall cling to his wife, and the two shall be made into one. This is a great mystery. I mean that it refers to Christ and the church. In any case, each one should love his own wife as he loves himself, the wife for her part showing respect for the husband (Eph 5:21–33).

Here I cannot attempt to comment at length on this passage.[42] Today this text is, unfortunately, not held in honor by some, who believe that it is demeaning to women insofar as it speaks of the wife's "submission" to her husband, who is characterized as her "head". My remarks here will be limited to the issues of submission and headship.

Pope John Paul II has, I believe, done much to help us understand this passage in its total context within the good news of salvation and in this way to appreciate properly the "submission" involved in marriage. In his commentary on this passage he first observes that the exhortation to husbands to love their wives as Christ loved the Church summons not only husbands but all men to be imitators of Christ in their dealings with women. And in Christ's love "there is a fundamental affirmation of the woman as person." Continuing, he then says:

> The author of the Letter to the Ephesians sees no contradiction between an exhortation formulated in this way and the words: "Wives, be subject to your husbands, as to the Lord. For the husband is the head of the wife" (Eph 5:22–23). The author knows that this way of speaking, so profoundly rooted in the customs and religious tradition of the time, is to be understood and carried out in a new way; as a *"mutual subjection out of reverence for Christ"* (cf. Eph 5:21). This is especially true because the husband is called the "head" of the wife *as* Christ is the head of the Church;

---

[42] A very perceptive and thoughtful commentary on this text is provided by Hans Urs von Balthasar, "Ephesians 5:21–33 and *Humanae Vitae*: A Meditation", in *Christian Married Love*, ed. Raymond Dennehy (San Francisco: Ignatius Press, 1981), pp. 55–73.

he is so in order to give "himself up for her" (Eph 5:25), and
giving himself up for her means giving up even his own life. However, whereas in the relationship between Christ and the Church
the subjection is only on the part of the Church, in the relationship between husband and wife the "subjection" is not one-sided
but mutual.[43]

From this it is clear that this passage in no way countenances
male domination nor does it impose on wives a one-sided subjection to their husbands. The intention of the sacred writer is to
call Christian husbands and wives to live their marriage relationship in mutual self-sacrifice, after the model of Christ.

With respect to the "headship" of the husband and of the father
in the family, I hold that there is a genuine truth, necessary for the
father-involved family, at stake. I will briefly attempt to show why.
First of all, there is need for authority in any human community.
Authority, however, must not be confused with domination and
the exercise of power; indeed, domination and the exercise of power
are abuses of authority. Authority is, rather, a necessary principle
of cooperation and thus a role of service to the community. Marriage and family life involve cooperative action and require uni-
fied decisions, and to make decisions is the proper task of authority
within marriage and the family, as it is within any human community.

Authority, in short, is not domination but decision-making. Husbands and wives surely share in this authority, which usually entails
common deliberation and often results in consensus. But at times
decision-making authority cannot be exercised in this way. Emergencies arise, when there is little or no possibility for common
deliberation and consent. At other times, consensus may not emerge.
Yet, for the common good of the marriage and of the spouses,
authority must be exercised by one or the other spouse. It seems
to me that here the complementary differences between male and
female are relevant and that these differences support the view that
the husband is the one who is required to exercise it.

This is commonly the case in emergency conditions. The identity of the one who is to exercise authority must be clear when

---

[43] *Mulieris dignitatem*, no. 24.

emergencies arise, and several attributes of the husband are crucial in such emergencies: his size and strength, his capacity for setting long-range goals and particular objectives for reaching them, his capacity for differentiating. When emergencies arise that require the cooperation of both spouses (and, at times, the children as well), the husband-father is often the one best suited to make and execute decisions. If authority in family emergencies pertains to the husband-father, it is fitting that he exercise it for the family as a whole in other instances when this is required—when cooperation is essential but no consensus can be reached. The proper exercise of this authority is by no means a matter of domination, but rather a gift to the marriage and to the family. In order for the husband to exercise his authority properly, he must be willing to be self-sacrificial and to subordinate his own individual interests to the well-being and good of the marriage and the family.[44] In this way he will manifest his love for his wife and reveal and relive on earth "the very fatherhood of God", ensuring "the harmonious and united development of all the members of the family".[45]

Conclusion

Marriage is the "creation of a lasting personal union between a man and a woman based on love".[46] It is a communion of persons intended to bear witness on earth and to image the intimate communion of persons within the Trinity.[47] It is a sacrament of the love-giving, life-giving bridal union between Christ and his Church, ordered to the procreation and education of children

[44] The considerations given here regarding the authority of the husband-father are developed more fully by Germain Grisez in *Living a Christian Life*, vol. 2 of his *The Way of the Lord Jesus* (Quincy, Ill.: Franciscan Press, 1993).

[45] *Familiaris consortio*, no. 25.

[46] Karol Wojtyla, *Love and Responsibility*, p. 218.

[47] On this matter, the excellent essay of Mary Rousseau is most helpful. See her "Pope John Paul II's *Letter on the Dignity and Vocation of Women*: The Call to Communio", *Communio: International Catholic Review* 16 (1989): 212–32.

who are to be lovingly received, nurtured humanely, and educated in the love and service of God.

This beautiful partnership, this wonderful covenant of love, unites human persons who differ in their sexuality and complement each other. Both husband and wife are to give and to receive; both are to image God as the "wellspring of the joy of living" and the "ocean depth of happy rest". But each is to do so in his and her indispensably complementary ways, the husband emphatically giving in a receiving sort of way and serving as the "wellspring of the joy of living", and the wife emphatically receiving in a giving sort of way and serving as the "ocean depth of happy rest". Their marital love, exclusive of others in the intimacy of their partnership of life and their one-flesh union, is the kind of love that is inclusive insofar as it reaches out to others and bears fruit in the world in which they live, as they joyously accept the gift of children and serve the needs of the society in which they live. The home based on the union of man and woman in Christian marriage is indeed a "domestic Church",[48] a witness to the truth that God is a loving Father and that the Church is our mother, and that all human persons, male and female, are called to love and communion.

---

[48] See *Lumen gentium*, no. 11; *Apostolicam actuositatem*, no. 11; *Familiaris consortio*, no. 49. See also CCC 1655–58 and 2204–6. Also, see below, Chapter Five.

3

Pope Paul VI: A True Prophet

The proper biblical and theological understanding of a prophet is that of a person who is an accredited witness of God's revelation, who can expound it rightly in the concrete situation facing him and his environment. Precisely because his appraisal of the issues confronting him and the people in the light of God's revelation requires him to consider the future, the prophet can interpret the present in view of its dynamism for the future—"prophecy" in the ordinary sense of the term today.[1]

Given this understanding of a prophet, I believe it is quite correct to regard Pope Paul VI as a true prophet and his encyclical *Humanae vitae* as a prophetic document. This was precisely the view of Pope John Paul II and others.[2] Paul VI was a prophet because he clearly affirmed central truths of human existence in the light of divine revelation, accurately assessed some of the major

[1] On this see Karl Rahner and Herbert Vorgrimler, *Dictionary of Theology*, 2nd ed. (New York: Crossroad, 1985), p. 419.

[2] See *Familiaris consortio*, no. 29, where John Paul II says: "Precisely because the love of husband and wife is a unique participation in the mystery of life and of the love of God Himself, the Church knows that she has received the special mission of guarding and protecting the lofty dignity of marriage and the most serious responsibility of the transmission of human life. Thus, in continuity with the living tradition of the ecclesiastical community throughout history, the recent Second Vatican Council and the magisterium of my predecessor Paul VI, expressed above all in the Encyclical *Humanae vitae*, have handed on to our times a truly prophetic proclamation, which reaffirms and reproposes with clarity the Church's teaching and norm, always old yet always new, regarding marriage and regarding the transmission of human life."

issues facing men and women of his—and our—day, and foresaw the terrible harms that human persons would suffer by abandoning God's design for marriage and the family.

To show the prophetic character of *Humanae vitae* I believe that it will be helpful, first of all (1), to consider the "integral vision" of human persons set forth in *Humanae vitae*, according to which there is an intimate and unbreakable bond uniting sex, love, and procreation, and, secondly (2), to examine the "disintegrative vision" of human persons underlying the acceptance of contraception, a vision dissolving this bond and, as a result, bringing to human persons the harms that Pope Paul feared would come about should God's plan for human existence be set aside. In conclusion, I will try to show the truth of Pope John Paul II's belief that the differences between these two "visions" is ultimately rooted in "two irreconcilable concepts of the human person and of human sexuality".[3]

1. The "Integral Vision" of Human Persons and the Bond Uniting Sex, Love, and Procreation

Paul VI wisely observed that the specific question taken up in *Humanae vitae*, namely, the most important mission [*munus*][4] of married men and women to hand on life to new human persons, can be addressed adequately only within the context provided by an "integral vision" of the human person, a vision illumined by

---

On the prophetic character of *Humanae vitae*, see the excellent book of Dionigi Tettamanzi *Un'Enciclica Profetica: La Humanae Vitae Vent'Anni Dopo* (Milan: Editrice Ancora Milano, 1988).

[3] *Familiaris consortio*, no. 32.

[4] On the rich meaning of the Latin term *munus*, used by Pope Paul VI to designate the "mission" of married couples to hand on life to new human persons, see Janet Smith, "The *Munus* of Transmitting Human Life: A New Approach to *Humanae vitae*", *The Thomist* 54 (July, 1990) 385–427. See also her *Humanae Vitae: A Generation Later* (Washington, D.C.: Catholic University of America Press, 1991), pp. 136–48.

divine revelation.⁵ In particular, he reminded us that this question must be examined in the light of God's plan for marriage and for human existence: "God the Creator wisely and providently established marriage with the intent that He might achieve His own design of love through men. Therefore, through mutual self-giving, which is unique [*proprium*] and exclusive to them, spouses seek a communion of persons [*personarum communionem*]. Through this communion, the spouses perfect each other so that they might share with God the task [*operam socient*] of procreating and educating new living beings."⁶

In this passage Pope Paul VI speaks of the "mutual self-giving ... unique and exclusive" to spouses. Marriage, as we have emphasized in earlier chapters, comes to be only when a man and a woman, by an act of irrevocable personal consent, give themselves to one another unreservedly and unconditionally. Their marital union is consummated and expressed in the act which is unique and exclusive to them, the marital act. Later in the Encyclical, speaking of the marital act, Paul VI has this to say: "because of its intrinsic nature [*intimam rationem*] the conjugal act, which unites husband and wife with the closest of bonds, also makes them *fit* to bring forth new life according to the laws written into their very nature as male and female."⁷ This is a remarkable and profoundly true statement. Married men and women, like unmarried men and women, have the *capacity*, by virtue of being endowed with genital organs, of generating new human life. But this capacity does not make them "fit" or "worthy" to bring forth new life "*according to the laws written into their very nature as male and female*". It is rather, according to Paul VI, the *conjugal act*, unique and

⁵ *Humanae vitae*, no. 7; in this chapter, except where noted, I am using the translation of *Humanae vitae* from the Latin text as provided by Janet Smith in her *Humanae Vitae: A Generation Later*. Note 7 of *Humanae vitae* is found on pp. 276–77 of her book.

⁶ Ibid., no. 8; Smith translation, pp. 277–78.

⁷ Ibid., no. 12. Here I do *not* follow the Smith translation or, in this instance, "mistranslation". According to Smith's translation (and that also of the Vatican), Paul said that the conjugal act "makes them [the spouses] *capable* of bringing forth new life. . . ." But the official Latin text does *not* say this. Rather it says that the conjugal act "eos *idoneos* facit", that is, "makes them *fit* or *worthy*".

exclusive to spouses, that makes them *fit* or *worthy* [*idoneos*] to do this. As I now hope to show, this is a sublime truth which greatly helps us to see the wisdom of "God's plan" for human existence.

Although human life, no matter how it comes to be, must be recognized and respected as sacred from the first moment of conception,[8] God does not will that new human life come to be through the random copulation of unmarried males and females. As we saw in Chapter One, unmarried men and women have no right to generate human life through their acts of fornication simply because they have not, through their own free choice, capacitated themselves to receive such life lovingly, nourish it humanely, and educate it in the love and service of God; they have not capacitated themselves to cooperate with God in raising up new human persons "according to the laws written into their very nature as males and females".[9]

Nor do unmarried males and females have a "right" to copulate. They do not have this right because they have refused, by their own free choice, to capacitate themselves to respect each other as irreplaceable and nonsubstitutable persons in their freely chosen acts of fornication. Those acts cannot unite a man and a woman who love and respect each other as irreplaceable and nonsubstitutable persons; all they can do is join *two individuals who are in principle replaceable, substitutable, disposable.*

But husbands and wives have the right to the marital act, the act which "makes them capable of bringing forth new life according to the laws written into their very nature as male and female".

---

[8] On this see John XXIII, Encyclical *Mater et magistra*, AAS 53 (1961): 447; cited explicitly by Paul VI in *Humanae vitae*, no. 13, note 13. See also *Gaudium et spes*, no. 51.

[9] Centuries ago St. Augustine put this beautifully, when he said that children are "to be lovingly received, nourished humanely, and educated religiously", i.e., in the love and service of God. See his *De genesi ad literam*, 9.7; PL 34:397. And children, as he rightly insisted, are a *good*, a *blessing* of marriage, which God established precisely so that "the chastity of women would make children known to their fathers and fathers to their children. True, it was possible for men to be born of promiscuous and random intercourse with any women at all, but there could not have been a bond of kinship between fathers and children." *Contra Julianum*, 5.9; PL 44:806.

They have the right to this act precisely because they have, through their own free and self-determining choice, given themselves to one another in marriage through an act of irrevocable personal consent—whereby they established each other as absolutely irreplaceable and nonsubstitutable persons.[10] By giving themselves to one another in marriage, husbands and wives have capacitated themselves to give one another conjugal love and to receive human life lovingly from God, to nourish it humanely, and to educate it in his love and service.

The marital act as a moral and human act, moreover, is not simply a genital act between a man and woman who *happen* to be married. As we saw earlier, in Chapter One, the marital act, as a human, moral act, is an act that inwardly participates in the one-flesh, marital union of husband and wife and in the "goods" or "blessings" of marriage, i.e., the goods of loving fidelity and of children. The *marital* act, therefore, as distinct from a mere *genital* act, is one that is (1) open to the communication of spousal love and (2) open to God's gift of new human life, the "supreme gift of marriage".[11]

Paul VI himself indicates the difference between a marital act as a moral and human act and a "marital" act understood purely descriptively as a genital act between a man and a woman who "happen" to be married. In a singularly perceptive passage he writes: "People rightly understand that a conjugal act [i.e., a marital act in the purely descriptive sense] imposed on a spouse, with no consideration given to the condition of the spouse or to the legitimate desires of the spouse, is not a true act of love. They understand that such an act opposes what the moral order rightly requires from spouses", that is, they understand that such an act does not truly participate in the marriage itself and in the "goods" of marriage. Quite to the contrary, it violates the goods of marital unity and friendship.[12] He goes on to say: "To be consistent, then, if they reflect further, they should acknowledge that it is

---

[10] On this see Vatican Council II, *Gaudium et spes*, no. 48; John Paul II, *Familiaris consortio*, no. 11. Also see above, Chapter One.

[11] *Gaudium et spes*, no. 49.

[12] *Humanae vitae*, no. 13; Smith translation, pp. 281–82.

necessarily true that an act of mutual love that impairs the capacity of bringing forth life contradicts both the divine plan that established the nature [*normam*] of the conjugal bond and also the will of the first Author of human life. For this capacity of bringing forth life was designed by God, the Creator of all, according to [his] specific laws." [13] An act of this kind, although "marital" in a purely descriptive sense, does not, like an act of spousal abuse, participate inwardly in the marriage and in the "goods" of marriage. To the contrary, an act of this kind violates the marital good of procreation because the spouses have, through their own free choice, shut it off, "closed" it, to God's gift of children.

Precisely because the marital act, as a human and moral act, is open both to the expression of spousal love and to the reception of God's gift of life to new human persons, there is inherent in it, as Pope Paul VI affirmed, "an unbreakable bond, established by God, which man is not permitted to break on his own initiative, between its unitive meaning and its procreative meaning".[14] There is, in short, a bond uniting sex, love, and the procreation of new human life. And what God has joined together, let no man put asunder.

Moreover, because every human person is a being made in God's image and likeness and is called to a life in union with God in Christ, *no human person ought ever to be unwanted, that is, unloved.* And to secure a society in which all human persons, including children, are indeed wanted and loved, it is absolutely imperative that men and women respect the bond uniting sex, love, and the transmission of human life, that they honor marriage and the marriage bed (cf. Heb 13:4), and open their hearts and homes to God's gift of children by letting the little children come to him (cf. Lk 18:15–16).

Thus contraception is an intrinsically immoral act precisely because it severs the bond uniting sex, love, and the procreation of human life. It is, indeed, an *anti-life* kind of act, through which men and women deliberately "close" their freely chosen acts of

[13] Ibid., no. 13.

[14] Ibid., no. 11. Here I have not followed the Smith translation. See also Pius XII, Address to Participants in the Second Naples World Congress on Fertility and Human Sterility, May 19, 1956; AAS 48 (1956): 470.

intimate union to God's gift of life.[15] The anti-life nature of contraception is evident from a consideration of what contraception
is. Pope Paul VI accurately described the nature of contraception
by identifying it as "every action, which, either in anticipation of
the conjugal act [or indeed of any genital act], or in its accomplishment, or in the development of its natural consequences, proposes [*intendat*], either as end or means, to impede procreation
[*ut procreatio impediatur*]".[16] In other words, what one does when

---

[15] On this see Germain Grisez, Joseph Boyle, John Finnis, and William E.
May, "'Every Marital Act Ought to Be Open to New Life': Toward a Clarification", *The Thomist* 52 (1988): 367–426. In *Humanae Vitae: A Generation Later*, Janet
Smith considers this argument "inadequate" and a departure from the Catholic
tradition. For a critique of her work, in which I show how she has, unfortunately, misunderstood our argument and has also failed to take into account the
traditional Catholic understanding of contraception as an anti-life act, see my
review of her book in the *The Thomist* 57 (1993): 155–61. On the traditional
understanding of contraception as anti-life, see the following note.

[16] *Humanae vitae*, no. 14. Here I have not used Janet Smith's translation because
she translates the Latin word *intendat* as "chooses". Paul VI, however, was definitely using this Latin term in the senses in which it was used by St. Thomas, as
designating *both* the intending of the end (*voluntas intendens*) *and* the choosing of
means (*voluntas eligens*), as the text of Paul VI makes clear, since he speaks of
"intending" or "proposing" to impede procreation either as one's *end* or *means*.

Pope Paul VI himself stressed the anti-life character of contraception in a homily given ten years after the publication of *Humanae vitae*: Homily on the Feast of
Ss. Peter and Paul, June 29, 1978 (AAS 70 [1978]: 397; printed in *L'Osservatore
Romano*, English ed., July 6, 1978), p. 3. Here he refers to *Humanae vitae* as a
defense of life "at the very source of human existence", a document which "drew
its inspiration from the inviolable teaching of the Bible and the Gospel, which
confirms the norms of the natural law and the unsurppressible dictates of con-
science on respect for life, the transmission of which is entrusted to responsible
fatherhood and motherhood". Moreover, in footnote 14 of *Humanae vitae* he explicitly referred to the teaching of the *Roman Catechism* (popularly known as *The
Catechism of the Council of Trent*), which was universally used in the Church from
the end of the sixteenth century until the middle of the last century, in which
contraception, like abortion, is branded an anti-life, homicidal kind of act. The
Roman Catechism affirmed that "whoever, joined in marriage, either impede conception by medicines or expel the child conceived, commit a most grave crime,
for this must be considered the impious conspiracy of homicides" (part II, chap. 8,
no. 13: the Latin text reads: "Fit ut illorum sit scelus gravissimum qui, Matrimonio iuncti, medicamentis vel conceptum impediunt, vel partum abigunt, haec

one contracepts is to impede, deliberately and intentionally, the beginning of a new human life. A person contracepts only because he or she, wishing to engage in genital sex—an act reasonably held to be the kind of act through which a new human life can come to be—does not want that new human life to come to be. Therefore, he or she does something prior to this freely chosen genital act, during it, or after it, precisely to impede or prevent that new human life from beginning. Should a new human life begin despite one's contraceptive efforts to impede its beginning, it comes to be as an "unwanted child", as St. Augustine noted in his *Confessions*, when, despite the contraceptive acts which he and his mistress engaged in, a child was conceived and born "against their wills".[17]

Moreover, when contraception is practiced by married couples, it is not only an anti-life kind of act, but an anti-love kind

---

enim homicidarum impia conspiratio existimanda est." The teaching of this catechism, in turn, is rooted in the centuries' old canon, the *Si aliquis*, which formed part of the Church's universal law from the thirteenth century until 1917: "If anyone for the sake of fulfilling sexual desire or with premeditated hatred does something to a man or to a woman, or gives something to drink, so that he cannot generate, or she cannot conceive, or offspring be born, let it be held as homicide" (Latin text: "Si aliquis causa explendae libidinis vel odii meditatione homini aut mulieri aliquid fecerit, vel ad potandum dederit, ut non possit generare, aut concipere, vel nasci soboles, ut homicida teneatur"). Text in *Decret. Greg. IX*, lib. V, titl. 12, cap. v; *Corpus iuris canonici*, ed. A.L. Richter and A. Friedberg (Leipzig: Tauchnitz, 1881), 2.794.

John Paul II has often noted the anti-life nature of contraception. See, for example, his homily at Mass for Youth, Nairobi, Kenya, August 17, 1985; *Insegnamenti di Giovanni Paolo II*, 8.2 (Rome: Libreria Editrice Vaticana, 1985), 453; printed in *L'Osservatore Romano*, English ed., August 26, 1985, p. 5. In this homily, after pointing out that the fullest sign of self-giving is when couples willingly accept children and quoting *Gaudium et spes*, 50, John Paul II says: "That is why anti-life actions such as contraception and abortion are wrong and are unworthy of good husbands and wives."

The anti-life character of contraception is also clearly noted in the *Catechism of the Catholic Church* (CCC), which affirms that "the Church, which 'is on the side of life' [*Familiaris consortio*, no. 30], teaches that 'each and every marriage act must remain open to the transmission of life' [*Humanae vitae*, no. 11]" (CCC 2366).

[17] St. Augustine, *Confessions*, bk. IV, chap. 2.

of act. By dissolving the bond uniting the unitive and procreative meanings of the conjugal act, contraception, as John Paul II and others have pointed out, "alters the value of 'total' self-giving". Through contraception "the innate language that expresses the total reciprocal self-giving of husband and wife is overlaid ... by an objectively contradictory language, namely, that of not giving oneself totally to the other. This leads not only to a positive refusal to be open to life but also to a falsification of the inner truth of conjugal love, which is called upon to give itself in personal total-ity." [18] Indeed, they change the moral character of the act of gen-ital union. It is no longer a "marital act" in the human, moral sense, for it no longer participates inwardly in the marriage and in the goods or blessings of marriage. It is deliberately closed both to the full-giving characteristic of marital love and to God's gift of life.

It is important to understand that the two meanings of the marital act, the unitive and the procreative, do not lie side-by-side as it were, stuck together, but are even closer than that: the life giving aspect of the marital act is *part* of its love-giving mean-ing. The two are inseparable because *no whole can be without its essential parts.*[19] The *Catechism of the Catholic Church* expresses this

[18] *Familiaris consortio*, no. 32. The *Catechism of the Catholic Church* (2370) makes this teaching of Pope John Paul II its own. John Paul II, who foreshadowed this line of argumentation in his *Love and Responsibility*, written originally in 1960 and translated into English in 1981 (New York: Farrar, Straus, Giroux, 1981; reprinted, San Franciso: Ignatius Press, 1993), developed it beautifully in his Wednesday audi-ences devoted to the development of a "Theology of the Body". His thought on this issue is presented accurately and attractively by Smith in *Humanae Vitae: A Generation Later*, pp. 107-18, 230–65.

[19] On this see Germain Grisez, *The Way of the Lord Jesus*, vol. 2, *Living a Chris-tian Life* (Quincy, Ill.: Franciscan Press, 1993), pp. 633–36. See also Francis X. Meehan, "Contemporary Theological Developments on Sexuality", in *Human Sexuality and Personhood* (St. Louis: Pope John XXIII Center, 1981), p. 177: "Sex-uality implies by its very bodily phenomenon a human-life dimension. What is often not understood, and what I would like to emphasize here, is that life and love are really not two separate meanings but are inherently connected and mutu-ally conditioned. For this reason *Humanae vitae* is more than a teaching on birth control: it is an anthropological insight suggesting that love calls for life—indeed so much so that any lack of orientation toward life actually flaws the love."

profound truth by saying: "A child does not come from outside as something added on to the mutual love of the spouses, but springs from the very heart of that mutual giving, as its fruit and fulfillment." [20]

Thus, central to the "integral vision" of human existence, rooted in divine revelation, at the heart of Pope Paul VI's prophetic encyclical is the truth that there is an inherent bond uniting sex, love, and procreation. The goods, the blessings, of human sexuality are love and life; the union of husbands and wives, like the union of Christ with his Church, is a life-giving, love-giving union that welcomes new human life as a precious gift from God.

2. The "Disintegrative Vision" of Human Persons and the Dissolving of the Bond Uniting Sex, Love, and Procreation

Yet this truth, unfortunately, has been cast aside today by many and in its place we find a vision of human sexuality and of human persons that has torn asunder the intrinsic bond uniting sex, love, and the handing on of human life. This understanding—or, more accurately, this terrible *mis*understanding—of human sexuality and of human persons is exactly the misunderstanding of human sexuality undergirding the widespread acceptance of contraception.

The noted biologist Ashley Montagu well expressed the new, contraceptive vision of human sexuality in an essay, written about the same time as *Humanae vitae*, in which he celebrated the discovery of the "pill", likening it to the discovery of fire and the invention of the wheel. According to Montagu, "the pill makes it possible to render every individual of reproductive age completely responsible for both his sexual and his reproductive behavior. *It is necessary*", he wrote, "*to be unequivocally clear concerning the distinction between sexual behavior and reproductive behavior.* Sexual behavior may have no purpose other than pleasure ... without the slightest intent of reproducing, or it may be indulged in for

[20] CCC 2366.

both pleasure and reproduction."[21] Or, to put it another way, "making love" is one thing, "making babies" is another.

On this view there is no longer any need, as there was in the whole past history of the race, to be overly concerned about "reproducing" in an act of genital sex. Thanks to the pill and other developments in contraceptive technology, mankind has been liberated from this fear. Indeed, the taboos imposed on sexual behavior in the past because of its association with reproduction no longer need to inhibit human choices. On this view it is obvious that the most frequent and durably most important meaning of sexual union consists in its ability to help human persons fulfill their need for orgasmic pleasure and to communicate affection.[22]

This mentality gives rise to the slogan, very popular and unquestionably accepted by most people in our culture, that "no unwanted child ought ever to be born." To prevent the tragedy of the birth of an "unwanted child" it is obviously imperative to have recourse to contraception and, should contraception fail, to abortion. But, on the other hand, persons who ardently desire a child ought to be able to have one, even if this means "producing" the child in the laboratory by in vitro fertilization and other techniques of "artful babymaking".[23] On this view, children become objects of human desire, "wanted" if desired, "unwanted" if not desired.

[21] Ashley Montagu, *Sex, Man, and Society* (New York: G. P. Putnam's, 1969), pp. 13–14; emphasis in the original.

[22] On this see the perceptive comments of George Gilder, *Sexual Suicide* (New York: Quadrangle Books, 1973), p. 34.

[23] Joseph Fletcher expresses this view quite lucidly. He writes: "Man is a maker and a selector and a designer, and the more rationally contrived and deliberate anything is, the more human it is. Any attempt to set up an antimony between natural and biological reproduction, on the one hand, and artificial and designed reproduction, on the other, is absurd. The real difference is between accidental or random reproduction and rationally willed or chosen reproduction.... It [the latter] is willed, chosen, purposed, and controlled, and surely these are among the traits that distinguish *homo sapiens* from others in the animal genus, from the primates down. Genital reproduction is, therefore, less human than laboratory reproduction, more fun, to be sure, *but with our separation of baby-making from love-making* both become more human because they are matters of choice, not chance." In "Ethical Aspects of Genetic Controls", *New England Journal of Medicine* 285 (1971): 781–82, emphasis added.

Their generation is transformed from an act of procreation to one of reproduction. They are treated, not as persons equal in dignity to their parents, but as products subordinated to the desires of their producers and subject to quality controls and cast aside if discovered to be "defective".

This contraceptive, disintegrative vision of human sexuality locates the human and personal value of sex in its relational purposes, in its ability to help people escape from the prison of loneliness and to enter into meaningful relationships with significant others and, in so doing, to enjoy themselves and find refreshment and ecstasy.[24] The procreative character of human sexuality, or, as advocates of contraception prefer to say, the "reproductive" aspect of human sexuality, is considered to be, of itself, subpersonal and subhuman, *becoming* personal and human only when "assumed into the human sphere", i.e., by being consciously willed and chosen.[25]

It logically follows, when the human significance of sex is seen in this way, that the principal criterion for evaluating sexual activity focuses on the quality of the relationship established and/or expressed by such activity. Thus, while hardly anyone in our

---

[24] This is clearly the way human sexuality is understood in contemporary American culture and by such influential secular writers as Montagu, Alex Comfort (author of *The Joy of Sex*), Dr. Ruth Westheimer (author of *Sex for Dummies*), and others. But this is also the way dissident Catholic theologians understand human sexuality. See, for example, Christine Gudorf, *Body, Sex, and Pleasure: Reconstructing Christian Sexual Ethics* (New York: 1994), her article "Contraception and Abortion in Roman Catholicism", in *Sacred Rights: The Case for Contraception and Abortion in World Religions*, ed. Daniel Maguire (Oxford: Oxford University Press, 2003), 55–78; Margaret Farley, *Just Love: A Framework for Christian Sexual Ethics* (New York: Continuum, 2006). Also see Louis Janssens, the noted Belgian theologian who for many years was professor of moral theology at Louvain University: "Considerations on Humanae Vitae", *Louvain Studies* 2 (1969): 249. According to Janssens, "the most profound meaning of human sexuality is that it is a relational reality, having a special significance for the person in his relationships." See also Kosnik et al., *Human Sexuality*.

[25] On this see one of the "Majority Report" of the Papal Commission on Population, the Family, and Natality, *Documentum Syntheticum de Paternitate Responsabili*, trans. as "The Question Is Not Closed", in *The Birth Control Debate*, ed. Robert Hoyt (Kansas City: *National Catholic Reporter*, 1968), p. 71.

contraceptive culture commends callous, cruel, or exploitative sexual activity, the opinion is pervasive that any kind of genital activity is permissible so long as it is "responsible". By this is meant genital activity that is caring and sensitive to the needs of the partner and that safeguards against sexually transmitted diseases such as herpes, AIDS, and unwanted pregnancies.

There is no need, on this view, for sexual partners to be married, although this may be considered as the ideal. In fact, there is no need that they be of opposite sex, for after all, homosexually oriented persons, male and female, have the same need for communicating affection and relieving sexual tensions through orgasm as do heterosexually oriented individuals. Indeed, there is today the claim that the "holy unions" of committed homosexuals be granted the same status as heterosexual marriages.[26]

What all this shows us is that, as Paul VI clearly foresaw in his prophetic encyclical, once the reasons alleged to justify contraception are accepted, there would follow a "gradual weakening in the discipline of morals". Surely prophetic was his admonition that "not much experience is needed to understand human weakness and to comprehend that human beings, especially the young, are so susceptible to temptation that they need to be encouraged to keep the moral law. It is wrong to make it easy for them to violate this law."[27] Is it not true that today, in our contraceptive culture, chastity is considered obsolete, indeed, according to the American Civil Liberties Union (ACLU), an unconstitutional imposition of religious doctrine, and that our youth is being instructed in the use of condoms and other contraceptive techniques?

---

[26] See, for instance, Brent Hartinger, "A Case for Gay Marriage", in *Perspectives on Marriage*, ed. Kieran Scott and Michael Warren (New York: Oxford University Press, 1993), pp. 130–35. It is noteworthy that this essay, and others of a similar caliber, appears in an anthology specifically designed by the editors as a text for use in courses on the theology of marriage taught in Roman Catholic colleges and universities. See also Stephen Macedo, "Sexuality and Liberty: Making Room for Nature and Tradition", in David M. Eastlund and Martha Nussbaum, eds., *Sex, Preference, and the Family* (New York: Oxford, 1997), pp. 86–101.

[27] *Humanae vitae*, no. 17; Smith translation, p. 286.

In addition, as Paul VI also foresaw, acceptance of contraception *and the rationale given to justify it* quickly leads to marital infidelity, because it is reasonable to fear that "husbands who become accustomed to contraceptive practices will lose respect for their wives [and will come] to disregard their wife's psychological and physical equilibrium and use their wives as instruments for serving their own desires. Consequently they will no longer view their wives as companions who should be treated with attentiveness and love." [28] The fear expressed by Paul has surely come to pass. It is no accident, as researchers such as Robert T. Michael have noted, that a dramatic increase in divorce in our society accompanied the dramatic increase in the practice of contraception, practiced both by fornicating couples prior to marriage and by husbands and wives in marriage. [29]

Moreover, as Paul VI again warned, acceptance of contraception and its underlying ideology would put a "dangerous power" into "the hands of rulers who care little about the moral law. Would anyone blame those in the highest offices of the state for employing a solution [contraception] considered morally permissible for spouses seeking to solve a family difficulty, when they strive to solve certain difficulties facing the whole nation?" [30] Is it not true that today we find authorities resorting to enforced sterilization and the implanting of such contraceptive-abortifacient devices as Norplant in order to cope with serious social problems? And this is true not only of India and China but of many places in the United States.

The accuracy of Pope Paul's predictions of the consequences that would accompany widespread practice of contraception has certainly been demonstrated in the forty years since the encyclical appeared, as the empirical evidence referred to in the Introduction to this new edition of this book amply testifies.

Indeed, since contraception is an anti-life kind of act, it leads logically and inevitably to abortion as a backup of contraception,

[28] Paul VI, *Humanae vitae*, n. 17; Smith translation, pp. 285–86.

[29] Robert T. Michael, "Why Did the U.S. Divorce Rate Double within a Decade?" in *Research in Population Economics*, vol. 6 (Greenwich, Conn., JAI Press, 1988): 367–99.

[30] *Humanae vitae*, no. 17; Smith translation, p. 286.

and state authorities have not been adverse to compulsory abortion, as the situation in China makes evident.

Truly, Paul VI was a prophet and *Humanae vitae* a prophetic document.

Conclusion: Two Contradictory Visions of Human Persons

Champions of contraception—in particular revisionist Catholic theologians like Louis Janssens, Charles Curran, and others—regularly claim that the "integral vision" of *Humanae vitae* is "physicalistic" and that in its place they are developing a truly "personalistic" vision of human persons and human sexuality.[31]

The truth is that we are confronted by two different kinds of "personalism", for, as John Paul II has perceptively noted, the anthropologies upon which the "integral vision" of Paul VI and upon which the "disintegrative vision" of the champions of contracepiton rest present us with "irreconcilable concepts of the human person and of human sexuality".[32]

Paul VI's "integral vision", the vision constantly kept before our eyes by the Church, holds that human persons are *bodily beings*. When God created man, he did not create a "conscious subject" to whom he then, as an afterthought, gave a body. Rather, in creating man, "male and female he created them" (Gen 1:27)—that is, as bodily, sexual beings. Moreover, when God the Son became man, he became *flesh* (*sarx egeneto*; Jn 1:14). Precisely because human persons are *bodily beings, body persons*, their sexuality, *including* its procreative power "wondrously surpasses the endowments of lower forms of life".[33] According to this

---

[31] See the following: Janssens, "Considerations on *Humanae Vitae*", 231–53; Janssens, "Norms and Priorities in a Love Ethic", *Louvain Studies* 6 (1977), 207–38; Charles Curran, "Sexual Ethics: A Critique", in his *Issues in Sexual and Medical Ethics* (Notre Dame, Ind.: University of Notre Dame Press, 1978), 30–51. See also Kosnik et al., *Human Sexuality*.

[32] *Familiaris consortio*, no. 32.

[33] *Gaudium et spes*, no. 51; see also Paul VI, *Humanae vitae*, nos. 10, 13; John Paul II, *Familiaris consortio*, no. 11.

integral vision of the human person, a living human body is a person, and every living human body, born or preborn, consciously aware of itself or crippled by severe mental handicaps so that it is not capable of consciousness, is a *person*, a being of surpassing goodness. Bodily life, in this vision, is not a merely instrumental good *for* the person, merely a condition for higher personal values, but is itself integral to the person and thus a good *of* the person.

Far different is the "personalism" of those who accept the "distintegrative vision" underlying the acceptance and practice of contraception. According to this "personalism", as we have seen, the procreative (or "reproductive") aspect of our sexuality is, of itself, merely a biological given, which needs to be "assumed into the human sphere" in order to *become* truly human and personal.[34] According to this vision, human persons are, in essence, "subjectivities", i.e., conscious selves aware of themselves as selves and capable of relating to other selves. Bodily life is a condition for personal life, and when personal life (i.e., consciously experienced life) has been irretrievably lost or will never emerge because of severe brain damage, bodily life is no longer a good, but, as one of the revisonist theologians puts it, "an excessive hardship".[35] In his magnificent Encyclical on certain fundamental questions concerning the Church's moral teaching, Pope John Paul II repudiated this dualistic position, comparing it to "certain ancient errors [gnosticism, Manichaeanism] ... always opposed by the Church".[36]

According to the "disintegrative vision" of human persons, moreover, a marriage "dies" when there is no longer any consciously experienced love between the spouses. Thus, the marriage simply is no longer, and one can no longer attribute indissolubility to what is nonexistent and the partners of this dead marriage are

---

[34] See "The Question Is Not Closed", p. 71.

[35] See Richard McCormick, "To Save or Let Die: The Dilemma of Modern Medicine", in *How Brave a New World?* (Garden City, N.Y.: Doubleday, 1978), p. 347.

[36] Pope John Paul II, *Veritatis splendor*, no. 49.

then free to marry again.[37] Pope Benedict XVI, while still Joseph Cardinal Ratzinger, commenting on this "vision" of person-hood, accurately pointed out that this understanding of human persons is rooted in the uncritical acceptance of an anthropology that ignores the deeper dimensions of human life and experience, *limiting the real and important simply to whatever may be occupying conscious thinking and living at the present moment.*[38]

The dualistic understanding of human persons and human sex-uality, so evident in this "disintegrative vision" of sex, love, and procreation, claims to liberate the person from biological laws in order to free him for the enjoyment of personal and interper-sonal values. But in reality, as Germain Grisez points out, it "alien-ates the human person from his or her own bodily reality". He continues:

> Thus Christian moral thought must remain grounded in a sound anthropology which maintains the bodiliness of the person. Such moral thought sees personal biological, not merely generically ani-mal biological, meaning and value in human sexuality. The bodies which become one flesh in sexual intercourse are persons; their unity in a certain sense forms a single person, the potential pro-creator from whom the personal, bodily reality of a new human individual flows in material, bodily, personal continuity. An attack on this biological process is an attack on the personal value of life . . . in its moment of tradition.[39]

Truly Pope Paul is a prophet. He upholds the priceless truth that human beings are bodily persons and that there is indeed an

[37] On this see Richard McCormick, S.J., "Notes on Moral Theology 1975", reprinted in *Notes on Moral Theology 1965–1980* (Washington, D.C.: University Press of America, 1980), pp. 544–60; Bernard Häring, "Internal Forum Solutions to Insoluble Marriage Cases", *The Jurist* 30 (1970): 22.

[38] Joseph Ratzinger, "Zur Frage nach der Unauflöslichkeit der Ehe", in *Ehe und Ehescheidung*, ed. F. Heinrich and E. Eid (Munich: Akademie-Schriften, 1972), pp. 49–50.

[39] Germain Grisez, "Dualism and the New Morality", in *Atti del Congresso Internazionale (Roma-Napoli, 17–14 aprile 1974): Tomasso D'Aquino nel Suo Settimo Centenario*, vol. 5, *L'Agire Morale*, ed. M. Zalba (Naples: Edizioni Domeni-cane Italiane, 1977), pp. 329–30.

intimate, unbreakable bond between sex, love, and procreation. He reminds us that every human person, born or unborn, ought to be wanted and loved, and that babies are not things to be wanted or unwanted, but God's gift, indeed, the supreme gift of marriage. It is time for men and women to shape their choices and actions in accord with the truth proclaimed in *Humanae vitae*.

4

"Begotten, Not Made": Catholic Teaching on the Laboratory Generation of Human Life

Introduction

The first child to be born after being conceived in vitro and not in her mother's body was Louise Brown. It is paradoxical, in my opinion, that Louise was born on July 25, 1978, ten years to the day after Pope Paul VI's encyclical *Humanae vitae* was promulgated. Louise's birth, indeed, her conception, would not have been possible had a technology separating "baby making" from "love making" not been developed. Yet a claim central to Pope Paul's encyclical was that "there is an unbreakable connection [*nexu indissolubili*] between the unitive meaning and the procreative meaning [of the conjugal act], and both are inherent in the conjugal act. This connection was established by God, and man is not permitted to break it through his own volition." [1]

Pope Paul's concern in *Humanae vitae* was with contraception and not with the laboratory generation of human life. But his teaching on the "unbreakable connection" between the two meanings of the conjugal act, as will be seen, plays a central role in the 1987 *Instruction on Respect for Human Life in Its Origin and on the Dignity of Procreation*—called *Donum vitae* in Latin—in which the Congregation for the Doctrine of the Faith formally addressed the moral issues raised by new reproductive technologies. This

[1] *Humanae vitae*, no. 12.

document, drawing on the understanding of marriage and human procreation found in the Catholic theological tradition, insists that the generation of human life, if it is to respect the dignity of both parents and children, "must be the fruit and sign of the mutual self-giving of the spouses, of their love and fidelity".[2]

In its treatment of heterologous fertilization, in which gametes, whether ova or sperm, from parties other than the spouses are used to generate new human life, the *Instruction*, not surprisingly, concludes that this way of generating human life is gravely immoral. It is so because such fertilization is "contrary to the unity of marriage, to the dignity of the spouses, to the vocation proper to parents, and the child's right to be conceived and brought into the world in marriage and through marriage".[3]

Although some find this judgment of the *Instruction* too restrictive of human freedom,[4] many people, Catholic and non-Catholic as well, can appreciate the reasons behind it, even if, in some highly unique situations, they might be ready to justify heterologous modes of generating human life. Nonetheless, they recognize that when a man and a woman marry they "give" themselves exclusively to each other and that the "selves" they give are sexual and procreative beings. Just as they violate their marital commitment by attempting, after marriage, to "give" themselves to another in sexual union,

[2] Congregation for the Doctrine of the Faith, *Instruction on Respect for Human Life in Its Origin and the Dignity of Procreation* (hereafter cited as the *Instruction*), part II, A, 1, with a footnote reference to *Gaudium et spes*, no. 50. The English text was printed in pamphlet form by Ignatius Press, San Francisco, Calif. (1987), and all references here will be to this edition. The material cited in the text is found on p. 22 of this edition.

[3] Ibid., II, A, 2, with a footnote reference to Pope Pius XII, Discourse to Those Taking Part in the Fourth International Congress of Catholic Doctors, September 29, 1949, *AAS* 41 (1949): 559.

[4] It should be noted that many people, particularly in affluent Western democracies such as the United States, where contraception has become a way of life, are favorably disposed to use of heterologous insemination and fertilization to help a childless couple have a baby, at least in some way, "of their own". Some, in fact, see the artificial generation of human life as "more human" than the "reproductive roulette" of generating children through sexual coition. See, for instance, Joseph Fletcher, *The Ethics of Genetic Control: Ending Reproductive Roulette* (Garden City, N.Y.: Doubleday Anchor Books, 1972).

so too they dishonor their marital covenant by freely choosing to exercise their procreative powers with someone other than their spouse, the person to whom they have given themselves, including their power to procreate, "forswearing all others".

But many of these same people, Catholic as well as non-Catholic, find the *Instruction's* teaching on the immorality of the "simple case" of in vitro fertilization and embryo transfer a different matter. In this case, there is no use of gametic materials from third parties; the child conceived is genetically the child of husband and wife, who are and will remain its parents. In this case, there need be no deliberate creation of "excess" human lives that will be discarded (perhaps through a procedure that some euphemistically call "pregnancy reduction"),[5] frozen, or made the objects of medical experimentations of no benefit to them. In this case there need be no intention to monitor the developing child *in utero* with a view toward its abortion should it develop some abnormality. Nor need there even be, in this case, the use of masturbation—a means judged intrinsically immoral by the Catholic Magisterium—in order to obtain the father's sperm, for his sperm can be retrieved in nonmasturbatory ways. In this case there is, apparently, only the intent to use modern technology as a means of helping a married couple, unable—either because of the wife's blocked fallopian tubes or the husband's low sperm production or other causes—to have a child of their own and give it a home where it can grow under the loving tutelage of its own parents. Many people, including several Catholic theologians, believe that recourse to in vitro fertilization and embryo transfer in this "simple case" is fully legitimate, since it does not seem to violate any one's rights but, to the contrary, seems to help a married couple's love blossom into life. They quite reasonably ask what is morally offensive here? What evil is being willed and done? Is not the

---

[5] "Pregnancy reduction" is the expression used by some doctors who deliberately kill within the womb "excess" children who have been conceived in vitro and implanted in their mother's wombs to enhance the likelihood that at least one child will survive pregnancy. Should all the embryos implanted continue development, and since multiple pregnancies raise some serious problems, the choice is made to resolve these problems by killing off excess and hence unwanted children.

Magisterium of the Church being too rigorous here? Is it not insensitive to the agony experienced by involuntarily sterile married couples who are simply seeking to realize one of the goods of marriage by making intelligent use of modern technology?

Here I will first present the principles set forth in the *Instruction* to support its conclusions. Since the *Instruction* does not, in general, seek to establish the truth of these principles or show their special place within the Christian view of human life, I will then attempt to show their truth and reasonableness.[6] Finally, I will consider some objections, raised by Catholic theologians, against the position taken by the *Instruction* on homologous in vitro fertilization and embryo transfer.

The Reasoning of the *Instruction*

The *Instruction* presents three principal lines of reasoning to support its conclusion that married couples ought not resort to in vitro fertilization and embryo transfer, even when the ovum comes

---

[6] Joseph Boyle, Jr., has written "An Introduction to the Vatican Instruction on Reproductive Technologies", *Linacre Quarterly* 55 (July 1988): 20–28; reprinted as "An Overview of the Vatican's Instruction on Reproductive Ethics" in *The Gift of Life: The Proceedings of a National Conference on the Vatican Instruction on Reproductive Ethics and Technology*, ed. Marilyn Wallace, R.S.M. and Thomas W. Hilgers, M.D. (Omaha, Neb.: Pope Paul VI Institute Press, 1990), pp. 19–26. References are to Boyle's work as reprinted in *The Gift of Life*. Boyle says that the most important principles underlying the *Instruction's* teaching can be expressed as five propositions. "First, God makes human individuals in His own image and likeness, and He is directly involved in the coming-to-be of each new person. Second, the human person is one being, bodily as well as spiritual, so bodily life and sexuality may not be treated as mere means to more fundamental purposes. Third, every living human individual, from the moment of conception, should be treated with the full respect due a person and so is inviolable. A human being is always a he or she, an I or a you, never an object, a mere something. Fourth, sexual activity and procreation can be morally good only if they are part of marital intercourse. Fifth, in marital intercourse, love-making and life-giving should not be separated" (p. 20). Boyle observes that in general the *Instruction* does not attempt to establish these principles, although it does provide some argumentation to support the principle requiring that all human individuals be treated as persons from the moment of conception (p. 21).

from the mother and the sperm used to fertilize it are retrieved in a morally acceptable way from her husband.

The first line of reasoning appeals to the "inseparability principle" that, as we have seen, is at the heart of Pope Paul's *Humanae vitae*. Applying this teaching to the issue of homologous artificial fertilization, the "simple case" with which we are concerned, the *Instruction* affirms, with Pope Pius XII, that "it is never permitted to separate these different aspects to such a degree as positively to exclude either the procreative intention [as is done in contraception] or the conjugal relation."[7] "Thus," the *Instruction* concludes,

> fertilization is licitly sought when it is the result of a "conjugal act which is *per se* suitable for the generation of children to which marriage is ordered by its very nature and by which the spouses become one flesh." But from the moral point of view procreation is deprived of its proper perfection when it is not desired as the fruit of the conjugal act, that is to say, of the specific act of the spouses' union.[8]

According to this line of reasoning, it is morally wrong for married couples to generate human life outside the marital act, because to do so is to choose to sever the bond between the unitive and procreative meanings of the conjugal act. But a willingness to do this, apparently, entails a willingness to deprive procreation of the goodness that it is meant to have as the fruit of the conjugal act.

A second argument presented in the *Instruction* to support its conclusion on the immorality of homologous in vitro fertilization and embryo transfer is based on the dignity of the child so conceived. The Vatican document insists that the child "cannot be desired or conceived as the product of an intervention of medical or biological techniques", inasmuch as "that would be the equivalent of reducing him to an object of scientific technology.

---

[7] *Instruction*, part II, B, 4, a, citing Pius XII, Discourse to Those Taking Part in the Second Naples World Congress on Fertility and Human Sterility, May 19, 1956, AAS 48 (1956): 470.

[8] Ibid., II, B, 4, a; emphasis in original document omitted. The internal citation is to the *Code of Canon Law*, can. 1061.

No one may subject the coming of a child into the world to conditions of technical efficacy which are to be evaluated according to standards of control and dominion."[9] But, the *Instruction* continues,

> Conception in vitro is the result of the technical action which presides over fertilization. Such fertilization is neither in fact achieved nor positively willed as the expression and fruit of a specific act of the conjugal union. In homologous IVF and ET, therefore, even if it is considered in the context of 'de facto' existing sexual relations, the generation of the human person is objectively deprived of its proper perfection: namely, that of being the result and fruit of a conjugal act in which the spouses can become "cooperators with God for giving life to a new person".[10]

The line of reasoning here can be summed up as follows: to desire or cause a child as a product of a technique is to make the child an object. But this is not compatible with the equality in personal dignity between the child and those who give it life.

A third line of reasoning is also given in the *Instruction* to support its conclusion. This line of reasoning is based on the "language of the body". According to the *Instruction*:

> Spouses mutually express their personal love in the "language of the body", which clearly involves both "spousal meanings" and parental ones. The conjugal act by which the couple mutually express their self-gift at the same time expresses openness to the gift of life. It is an act that is inseparably corporal and spiritual. It is in their bodies and through their bodies that the spouses consummate their marriage and are able to become father and mother.[11]

The document then continues,

> In order to respect the language of their bodies and their natural generosity, the conjugal union must take place with respect for its

[9] Ibid., II, B, 4, c.

[10] Ibid., II, B, 5. Emphasis in original omitted; the internal reference is to *Familiaris consortio*, no. 14; AAS 74 (1982): 96.

[11] *Instruction*, part II, B, 4, b. Emphasis in the original omitted, with a footnote reference to Pope John Paul II, General Audience of 16 January 1980, in *Insegnamenti di Giovanni Paolo II*, 3.1 (1980): 148–52.

openness to procreation; and the procreation of a person must be the fruit and result of married love. The origin of the human being thus follows from a procreation that is "linked to the union, not only biological but also spiritual, of the parents, made one by the bond of marriage." Fertilization achieved outside the bodies of the couple remains by this very fact deprived of the meanings and values which are expressed in the language of the body and in the union of married persons.[12]

According to this line of reasoning, in vitro fertilization, which occurs outside the body of the mother and independently of the bodily act by which spouses express their marital union in a unique and spousal way, is a way of generating human life that fails to respect the "language of the body". It is a mode of human generation that in no way acknowledges the deep human significance of the personal gift, bodily and spiritual in nature, of husband and wife to one another in the marital act.

It seems to me that the argument based on the "language of the body", one central to the Theology of the Body set forth by Pope John Paul II so extensively,[13] is intimately linked to the argument based on the "inseparability principle". Consequently, in what follows I will seek to show how these two lines of reasoning seem to merge and how closely they depend on a fundamental vision of marriage, the marital act, and the generation of human life.

Of the three lines of reasoning found in the *Instruction* to support its conclusion, I believe that the second, which rejects in vitro fertilization and embryo transfer on the grounds that generating human life in the laboratory is a form of production and demeans human life by treating it as if it were a product, provides the basis for the most straightforward argument against resorting to the laboratory generation of human life. Still the other two lines of reasoning, in my opinion, illumine the wider issues concerning human existence raised by new reproductive technologies. But to appreciate these lines of reasoning, it is first necessary

[12] Ibid., the internal citation is from Pope John Paul II, Discourse to Those Taking Part in the 35th General Assembly of the World Medical Association, October 29, 1983, AAS 76 (1984): 393.

[13] See *Man and Woman*; see also Chapter Six below.

to probe the meaning of marriage and the relationship between marriage, the marital act, and the generation of human life.

Marital Rights and Capabilities, the Marital Act, and the Generation of Human Life

Much that is said here recapitulates material set forth in Chapter One of this book. It may nonetheless be useful to summarize what was said there. By giving themselves to one another in marriage, husbands and wives not only acquire rights that nonmarried men and women do not have but also capacitate themselves to *do* things that nonmarried men and women are not capable of doing. Nonmarried men and women have the natural capacity, by virtue of their sexuality and endowment with sexual organs, to engage in genital sex and through it to generate human life. Yet they do not have the *right* either to engage in genital sex or to generate human life. Although here I cannot show fully why they do not have the right to engage in genital sex,[14] I can briefly indicate why. The reason is that they have not, by their own free, self-determining choice, capacitated themselves to respect each other as irreplaceable and nonsubstitutable persons in their freely chosen genital acts. When nonmarried men and women have sex, their genital act *does not unite two irreplaceable and nonsubstitutable persons* but rather *joins two individuals who are in principle replaceable and substitutable, disposable*. But human beings ought not to be treated as if they were replaceable, substitutable, disposable things. Similarly, nonmarried men and women do not have the right to generate human life precisely because they have not, through their own free choice, given themselves the capacity to receive such life lovingly, nourish it

---

[14] I have sought to defend the truth of this claim elsewhere. See, for instance, my *Sex, Marriage, and Chastity: Reflections of a Catholic Layman, Spouse, and Parent* (Chicago: Franciscan Herald Press, 1981), Chapter 5; "Sexual Ethics and Human Dignity", in *Persona, Verità e Morale: Atti del Congresso Internazionale di Teologia Morale (Roma, 7–12 aprile 1986)* (Rome: Città Nuova Editrice, 1988), pp. 477–95, in particular, pp. 488–89.

humanely, and educate it in the love and service of God and neighbor.[15]

But husbands and wives have the right to an intimate sharing of life and love and to the marital act, whose nature will be examined more fully below. They have this right precisely because they have capacitated themselves, through their irrevocable gift of themselves to one another in marriage,[16] to respect one another as irreplaceable and nonsubstitutable spouses. When they choose to unite in the marital act, this act truly unites two irreplaceable and nonsubstitutable persons. Similarly, they have capacitated themselves to receive human life lovingly, nourish it humanely, and educate it in the love and service of God and neighbor, for by their choice to marry they have made themselves capable of receiving any human life that might be given to them and of providing it with the home to which it has a right and in which it can take root and grow under the loving tutelage of its own father and mother, persons who are not strangers to one another but uniquely *one flesh* in marriage.

The marital act, as we have seen already, is not simply a genital act between a man and a woman who happen to be married. It is in truth an act that inwardly participates in their marital union; it is an act inwardly participating in the "goods" of marriage, i.e., the good of steadfast fidelity and of exclusive marital love and the good of children. The marital act is thus an act which is (1) open to the communication of spousal love and (2) open to the reception of new human life. A genital act forced upon a wife by a drunken husband seeking only to gratify his sexual urges and unconcerned with her legitimate desires is a genital act, but it cannot be regarded as a true marital act.[17] Similarly, in my opinion, a genital act between husbands and wives that is deliberately

---

[15] Centuries ago St. Augustine rightly and wisely noted that one of the principal goods of marriage is children, who are to be received lovingly, nourished humanely, and educated religiously. See his *De genesi ad literam*, 9.7 (PL 34:397).

[16] On this see, for example, *Gaudium et spes*, no. 48.

[17] It is worth noting here what Pope Paul VI had to say in *Humanae vitae*, no. 13. There he explicitly stated that a "conjugal act" (using the expression in a purely descriptive sense, to designate a genital act between individuals who happen

made hostile to the reception of human life, i.e., an act of contracepted intercourse, is also made to be *nonmarital* precisely because it is an act deliberately made inimical to one of the goods of marriage.[18]

The marital act, in other words, is by its own inner nature love-giving or unitive and open to the transmission of human life or procreative. And it is so precisely because it is *marital*, i.e., an act participating in marriage and the goods perfective of it. The bond, therefore, that unites the two meanings of the marital act is the marriage itself. But "what God has joined together, let no man put asunder." It is for this reason, I believe, that there is an "unbreakable connection between the unitive meaning and the procreative meaning" of the conjugal act.

The marital act is not, as Pope Pius XII rightly said, "a mere organic function for the transmission of the germs of life". To the contrary it is, as he noted, "a personal action, a simultaneous natural self-giving which, in the words of Holy Scripture, effects the union in 'one flesh' ... [and] implies a personal cooperation [of the spouses with God in giving new human life]."[19] Indeed, as Pope Paul VI put matters, "because of its intrinsic nature [*intimam rationem*], the conjugal act, which unites husband and wife with the closest of bonds, also makes them *fit* [*eos idoneos etiam facit*] for bringing forth new life."[20]

In addition, one can rightly say that the marital act speaks the "language of the body". It beautifully expresses the personal, bodily integrity of the spouses. To see what this means, I think that some observations by John Finnis concerning personal integrity

---

to be married) imposed by one of the spouses upon the other against the reasonable desires of the other violates the requirements of the moral order.

[18] On this question, which cannot, of course, be taken up adequately here, see Germain Grisez et al., "Every Marital Act Ought to Be Open to New Life". See above, Chapter Three.

[19] Pope Pius XII, Apostolate of the Midwives: An Address to the Italian Catholic Union of Midwives, October 29, 1951; text in *The Catholic Mind* 50 (1952): 61.

[20] *Humanae vitae*, no. 12.

are relevant. According to Finnis, "personal integrity involves . . . that one be reaching out with one's will, i.e., freely choosing real goods, and that one's efforts to realize these goods involves, where appropriate, one's bodily activity, so that that activity is as much the constitutive subject of what one does as one's act of choice is. That one really be realizing goods in the world; that one be doing so by one's free and aware choice, that that choice be carried into effect by one's own bodily action, including, where appropriate, bodily acts of communication and cooperation with other real people—these are the fundamental aspects of personal integrity."[21] In the marital act a husband and wife are indeed freely choosing and realizing real goods in the world—their own marital union and new human life. Their bodily activity is surely a constitutive subject of what they do; and cooperation with another is not only appropriate but necessary. The marital act is an utterly unique kind of human act; it is a collaborative, personal act carrying out the choice of the spouses to actualize their marriage and participate in the goods perfective of it.

Procreation vs. Reproduction

As we have just seen, when human life is given through the act of marital union, it comes, even when it is ardently desired, as a "gift" crowning the act itself. The marital act is not an act of "making", either babies or love. Love is not a product that one makes; it is a gift that one gives—the gift of self. Similarly, a baby is not a product inferior to its producers; it is, rather, a being equal in dignity to its parents. The marital act is surely something that husbands and wives "do"; it is not something that they "make". But what is the difference between "making" and "doing", and what bearing does this difference have on the issue of in vitro fertilization and embryo transfer?

[21] John Finnis, "Personal Integrity, Sexual Morality, and Responsible Parenthood", *Amhropos* (now *Anthropotes*) 1.1 (1985): 46.

In "making" the action proceeds from an agent or agents to something in the external world, to a product. Autoworkers, for instance, produce cars; cooks produce meals; bakers make cakes. Such action is transitive in nature because it passes from the acting subject(s) to an object fashioned by him or her (or them) and external to them. In making, which is governed by the rules of art, interest centers on the product made—and ordinarily products that do not measure up to standards are discarded; at any rate, they are little appreciated, and for this reason are frequently called "defective". Those who produce the products made may be morally good autoworkers or bakers or cooks or they may be morally bad, but our interest in "making" is in the product, not the producers, and we would prefer to have good cakes made by morally bad bakers than indigestible ones baked by saints who are incompetent bakers.

In "doing" the action abides in the acting subject(s). The action is immanent and is governed by the requirements of prudence, not art. If the action is morally good, it perfects the agent; if bad, it degrades and dehumanizes him or her.[22] It must be noted, moreover, that every act of making is also a doing insofar as it is freely chosen, for the choice to make something is something that we "do", and this choice, as self-determining, abides in us. Thus, in choosing to make a cake for someone's birthday, one is choosing to enhance the good of human friendship and is "doing" something good and making oneself to be, in this respect, a good person. Likewise, in choosing to make pornographic films, one is choosing to do something evil because it dishonors the dignity of human persons. There are, in other words, some things that we ought not to make, because choosing to make them is morally bad.

The marital act, as we have seen, is not an act of making. It is rather an act freely chosen by spouses to express their marital union, one open to the communication of marital love and to

[22] Classic sources for the distinction between making and doing are: Aristotle, *Metaphysics*, bk. 9, c. 8, 1050a23–1050b1; Thomas Aquinas, *In IX Metaphysicorum*, Lect. 8, n. 1865, *Summa theologiae*, I, q. 4, a. 2 ad 2; I, q. 14, a. 5 ad 1; I, q. 181, a. 1.

the transmission of human life. As such, the marital act is an act inwardly perfective of them and of their life as spouses, the life of which they are co-subjects, just as they are the co-subjects of the marital act itself. Even when they choose this act with the ardent hope that, through it, new human life will be given to them, the life begotten is not the product of their act but is a "gift supervening on and giving permanent embodiment to" the marital act itself.[23] When human life comes to be through the marital act, we can say quite properly that the spouses are "begetting" or "procreating". They are not "making" anything. The life they receive is "begotten, not made".

But when human life comes to be as a result of in vitro fertilization—whether heterologous or homologous—it is the end product of a series of actions, transitive in nature, undertaken by different persons. The spouses "produce" the gametic materials which others then use in order to make the final product, the child. In such a procedure the child "comes into existence, not as a gift supervening on an act expressive of the marital union ... but rather in the manner of a product of a making (and, typically, as the end product of a process managed and carried out by persons other than his parents)".[24] The life generated is "made", not "begotten".

But a child is not a product inferior to its producers and subject to quality controls (even if the choice is made not to apply these controls). It is, rather, as I have noted already, a person equal in dignity to its parents. A child, therefore, ought not to be treated as if it were a product. A child, therefore, ought not to be generated by in vitro fertilization, heterologous or homologous.

Advocates of homologous in vitro fertilization (IVF), including some Catholic theologians, reject this line of reasoning. As Richard McCormick says, "They do not see IVF as 'manufacture' of a 'product'. Fertilization *happens* when sperm and egg are brought together in a petri dish. The technician's 'intervention is

[23] Catholic Bishops Committee on Bioethical Issues, *In Vitro Fertilization: Morality and Public Policy* (London: Catholic Information Services, 1983), no. 23.

[24] Ibid., no. 24.

a condition for its happening; it is not a cause'." [25] Moreover, McCormick continues, "the attitudes of the parents and the technicians can be every bit as reverential and respectful as they would be in the face of human life naturally conceived." [26] Indeed, in McCormick's view (and in that of some other writers), homologous in vitro fertilization and embryo transfer can be considered an "extension" of intercourse, so that the child generated can still be regarded as the "fruit" of the spouses' love. While it is preferable, if possible, to generate the baby through the marital act, it is, in the cases we are concerned with, impossible to do so. Given the concrete situation, any disadvantages inherent in the generation of human lives apart from the marital act are clearly counterbalanced by the great good of new human lives and the fulfillment of the desire for children of couples who otherwise cannot have them. In this concrete situation, it is not unrealistic, so this line of thinking holds, to say that IVF is simply a way of "extending" the marital act.

Naturally, those who choose to produce a baby make that choice only as a means to an ulterior end. They may well intend that the baby be received into an authentic child-parent relationship, in which he will live in the communion which befits those who share personal dignity. If realized, this intended end for the sake of which the choice is made to produce the baby will be good for the baby as well as for the parents. But, even so, and despite McCormick's claim to the contrary, the baby's initial status is the status of a product. In in vitro fertilization the technician does not simply assist the marital act (that would be licit), but, as Benedict Ashley rightly notes, " '*substitutes*' for that act of personal relationship and communication one which is like a chemist making a compound or a gardener planting a seed. The technician has thus become the principal cause of generation, acting through

---

[25] Richard A. McCormick, S.J., *The Critical Calling: Reflections on Moral Dilemmas Since Vatican II* (Washington, D.C.: Georgetown University Press, 1989), p. 337; the internal citation is from William Daniel, S.J., "In Vitro Fertilization: Two Problem Areas", *Australasian Catholic Record* 63 (1986): 27.

[26] Ibid.

the instrumental forces of sperm and ovum." [27] Moreover, the claim that in vitro fertilization is an "extension" of the marital act and not a substitution for it is simply contrary to fact. "What is extended", as Ashley also notes, "is not the act of intercourse, but the intention: from an intention to beget a child naturally to getting it by IVF, by artificial insemination, or by help of a surrogate mother." [28]

Since the child's initial status in in vitro fertilization is that of a product, its status is subpersonal. Thus, the choice to produce a baby is inevitably the choice to enter into a relationship with the baby, not as an equal, but as a product inferior to its producers. But this initial relationship of those who choose to produce babies with the babies they produce is inconsistent with and so impedes the communion of persons endowed with equal dignity which is appropriate to any interpersonal relationship. It is the choice of a bad means to a good end. Moreover, in producing babies, if the product is defective, a new person comes to be as *unwanted*. Thus, those who produce babies not only choose life for some, but—does anyone doubt it?— quietly dispose at least some of those who are not developing normally.[29]

In short, human beings, who are the created words that the Uncreated Word of God became and is, ought, like the Uncreated Word, to be "begotten, not made". They are begotten in the marital act, a unique human act expressive of the marital union of husbands and wives and open to the generation of new human life; they are made in laboratories by in vitro fertilization, whether heterologous or homologous. Begetting is a personal act that, by its nature, cannot be "delegated" to others. Spouses can no more delegate to others the privilege they have of begetting human life

[27] Benedict Ashley, O.P., "The Chill Factor in Moral Theology", *Linacre Quarterly* 57.4 (November, 1990): 71.

[28] Ibid., 72.

[29] In the previous paragraphs, in addition to citing from Benedict Ashley, I have also paraphrased material developed by Grisez, Finnis, Boyle, and May in "Every Marital Act" (see footnote 18 above).

than they can delegate to others the right they have to engage in the marital act.[30]

[30] On this, see the thought-provoking comments of Janet Smith in her essay, "The Vocation of Christian Marriage as an Approach to the Bioethics of Human Reproduction", in *The Gift of Life*, pp. 49–60, and pp. 58–59.

The *Catechism of the Catholic Church* contains a brief but excellent section on the laboratory reproduction of human life (nos. 2376–78). This document quite rightly affirms: "A child is not something owed to one, but is a *gift*. The 'supreme gift of marriage' is a human person. A child may not be considered a piece of property, an idea to which an alleged 'right to a child' would lead. In this area, only the child possesses genuine rights: the right 'to be the fruit of the specific act of the conjugal love of his parents,' and 'the right to be respected as a person from the moment of his conception' [*Donum vitae*, II, 8]", CCC 2378.

5

The Christian Family:
A Domestic Church

In modern times the family was first referred to as the "domestic church" by the Fathers of Vatican Council II in the Dogmatic Constitution of the Church *Lumen gentium*, where they declared: "In what might be regarded as the domestic church [the Latin text reads: *In hac velut Ecclesia domestica parentes* ...], the parents, by word and example, are the first heralds of the faith with regard to their children" (*Lumen gentium*, no. 11). This re-introduction by the Fathers of Vatican II of an ancient understanding of the family was done with almost no explanation. The title "domestic church" was applied only in an analogous way to the Christian family ["*In hac velut Ecclesia domestica*"], and, as Joseph Atkinson has pointed out, with no developed theological grounding.[1]

It is instructive to note that in 1960, before the Council, Pope John Paul II as Cardinal Karol Wojtyla wrote a wonderful book on

---

[1] See Joseph Atkinson, "Family as Domestic Church: Developmental Trajectory, Legitimacy, and Problems of Appropriation", *Theological Studies* 66 (2005): 592–604, at p. 592. Atkinson (594–96) provides an interesting account, based on the *Acta synodalia Sacrosancti Concilii Oecumenici Vaticani II*, of the interventions of Bishop Pietro Fiordelli of Prato, Italy during debates over the text of *Lumen gentium* in which he said that parishes are divided into smaller holy cells, Christian families, "which we can call, following the example of the Holy Fathers, tiny churches" and spoke of the Christian family as a "small church possessing in itself a sharing of the very mystery of the union of Christ with the Church". Fiordelli's interventions undoubtedly led the Council Fathers to apply this term to the Christian family in the final text of *Lumen gentium*.

marriage and family, *Love and Responsibility*, in which he defined
the family as "an educational institution within the framework of
which the personality of a new human being is formed". In that
book he also referred to the family as "a small society, and the
existence of all large societies—nation, state, Church—depends
on it", and as "an institution based on marriage".[2] It was only *after*
his experience of Vatican II that he began his radical investigation
of the family, showing that the family's ecclesial dimension—its
being Church—is constitutive of its meaning.

Pope John Paul II's Teaching on the Domestic Church

In *Familiaris consortio*, which he himself describes as "a *summa* of
the teaching of the Church on the life, the tasks, the responsibilities, and the mission of marriage and the family in the world
today",[3] he gives us a rich understanding of the family as domestic church. He begins Part Three of this document (its longest
part and entitled "The Role of the Christian Family") with a
heading entitled, "Family, Become What You Are", And in its
first numbered section he declares:

> The family finds in the plan of God the Creator and Redeemer
> not only its *identity*, what it *is*, but also its *mission*, what it can and
> should *do*. The role that God calls the family to perform in his-
> tory derives from what the family *is;* its role represents the dynamic
> and existential development of what it is. Each family finds within
> itself a summons that cannot be ignored, and this specifies both its
> dignity and its responsibility: family *become* what you *are*.[4]

This is a very Pauline way of speaking, for St. Paul's basic mes-
sage to the Christian communities whom he evangelized was that

---

[2] *Love and Responsibility*, p. 217.

[3] Pope John Paul II, Address of December 22, 1981 in which he presented the
text of *Familiaris consortio*. Address "La Chiesa rinnova il dialogo con il mondo
per favorire la comprensione tra i popoli", in *Insegnamenti di Giovanni Paolo II* 4/2
(1981): 1215.

[4] *Familiaris consortio*, no. 17, italics added.

they should *become what they are*, that is, persons who have put on Christ, who have been sanctified by his Spirit, and regenerated as members of God's own family; thus they *are other Christs*.[5] For John Paul II the Christian family *is* the domestic church. Thus that is what it must *become*.

John Paul II taught that the family must be understood through the prism of its ecclesial and Christological identity. Families, he wrote, "will manifest to all people the Savior's living presence in the world, and the genuine nature of the Church",[6] Thus, as Atkinson correctly points out, "John Paul II situates the identity of the family along two axes: Christ and the Church." He then goes on to say:

In nos. 17–49, the bulk of the document, *Familiaris consortio* defines the family's essence and role as being "to guard, reveal and communicate love". This is not merely an amorphous phrase. It is further defined by its interior reference to Christ. "This is a . . . real sharing in God's love for humanity and the love of Christ the Lord for the Church his bride" (no. 17). It is this that reveals the ecclesiological [I would prefer *ecclesial*] nature of the family. John Paul II then divides this into four constitutive aspects: (1) forming a community of persons, (2) serving life, (3) participating in the development of society and, (4) sharing in the life and mission of the Church. These are marks of the Church and the family. If it truly shares in the life of the Church, the family cannot be separated from the Church but must be inserted into her very reality, thereby becoming true to its nature.

Immediately following this presentation, John Paul II begins to develop the second axis of the family: its relationship to Christ himself [its *christological* axis]. He writes that to understand the "substance" of the family we must do so "in reference to Jesus Christ as Prophet, Priest and King" (*Familiaris consortio*, no. 51). This is further expanded in terms of the family being (a) a believing and evangelizing community (prophetic nature); (b) a community in dialogue

---

[5] On this see George T. Montague, S.M., *Maturing in Christ: St. Paul's Program for Christian Growth* (Milwaukee: Bruce, 1962).

[6] *Familiaris consortio*, no. 60.

with God (priestly nature); and (c) a community at the service of man (kingly nature) (ibid., no. 50). *This means that the nature of the family is to be found in the nature of Christ.*[7]

Let us now examine how John Paul II presents the *ecclesial* and *christological* axes of the family as domestic church in *Familiaris consortio*.

The Ecclesial Axis

As noted, John Paul II emphasized that "the family has the mission to guard, reveal and communicate love, and this is a living reflection of and a real sharing of God's love for humanity and the love of Christ the lord for his bride, the Church." The mission to guard, reveal, and communicate love is entrusted to *every* human family, whether Christian or not, by virtue of its very being as a reality having God as its author, who even prior to his revelation of himself in Christ used the marriage of man and woman and the family based on this union as an image of his loving union with his people (cf. Hos 1–3).

But an even greater mission has been entrusted to the *Christian* family according to the plan of God the Redeemer. The family, as *Christian*, finds its origin, inner identity, and vocation in Christ and his bride, the Church. For it is the Church, as John Paul writes, that both "gives birth to ... the Christian family" and, "by proclaiming the word of God ... reveals to the Christian family its true identity, what it is and what it should be according to the Lord's plan".[8] Since the reality of the Christian family derives from its being generated by the Church, the identity of the Christian family is that of a "Church in miniature", summoned to "imitate and relive the same self-giving and sacrificial love that the Lord Jesus has for the entire human race", i.e., a redemptive, grace-giving kind of love. The Christian family thus participates in the very mystery of the Church.

Properly to understand what this means, it is necessary to consider how the Church as mother "gives birth" to the Christian

---

[7] Atkinson, "Family as Domestic Church", 599.

[8] *Familiaris consortio*, no. 49.

family. And to understand this we need to consider the relationship between baptism and marriage. The family is rooted in marriage, and marriage, as the Church has always taught, comes into
being only through the free, irrevocable consent of a man and
woman who, forswearing all others, freely give themselves to and
are freely received by one another as husband and wife. If the
man and the woman giving marital consent are Christians, this
means that they are *already* members of Christ's body, the Church;
they are persons who have *already*, through baptism, become indissolubly one with Christ and his spouse, the Church. As John
Paul II noted earlier in *Familiaris consortio*, "by means of baptism,
man and woman are definitively placed within the new and eternal covenant, in the spousal covenant of Christ with the Church." [9]
His point is that through baptism we become *new* persons, truly
children of God and brothers and sisters of Jesus, called—and
empowered—to love even as we have been and are loved by God
in Christ (cf. Jn 13:34; 15:12–14; 1 Jn 3:16). Through baptism we
"die" to sin and rise to a new kind of life in Christ; through
baptism we freely commit ourselves to live in union with Jesus
and to share in his redemptive work. Our vocation as Christians
is to complete, in our own flesh, "what is lacking in Christ's
afflictions for the sake of his body, that is, the Church" (Col 1:24).

Consequently, as John Paul II notes, "it is because of this indestructible insertion [of Christian men and women into the spousal covenant of Christ with the Church] that the intimate
community of conjugal life and love, founded by the Creator, is
elevated and assumed into the spousal charity of Christ, sustained
and enriched by His redeeming power." [10] It is for this reason
that the deepest identity of the Christian family is that of a "Church
in miniature (*Ecclesia domestica*)". [11] This identity is grounded in
the reality of Christian marriage as a true sacrament.

The Church's understanding of marriage as a sacrament in the
precise sense of a created, visible reality that signifies and makes

[9] Ibid., no. 13.
[10] Ibid.
[11] Ibid., no. 49.

efficaciously present in the world the invisible reality of God's redemptive grace is rooted in its understanding of Christian marriage as a reality that not only *signifies*, as do all true marriages, the life-giving, love-giving, grace-giving union of Christ with his bride the Church, but also *inwardly participates* in this union. It is precisely for this reason that the Christian family, rooted in the marriage of baptized men and women, is in truth a "Church in miniature".

Thus John Paul can rightly say that the marriage of Christian men and women "is the real representation, by means of the sacramental sign, of the very relationship of Christ with the Church".[12] From this it follows, moreover, that

> [Christian] spouses are therefore the permanent reminder to the Church of what happened on the Cross; they are for one another and for their children witnesses to the salvation in which the sacrament makes them sharers. Of this salvation event marriage, like every sacrament, is a memorial, actuation, and prophecy: "As a memorial, the sacrament gives them the grace and duty of commemorating the great works of God and of bearing witness to them before their children. As actuation, it gives them the grace and duty of putting into practice in the present, towards each other and their children, the demands of a love which forgives and redeems. As prophecy, it gives them the grace and duty of living and bearing witness to the hope of the future encounter with Christ."[13]

All Christians, whether married or not, have, through baptism, freely committed themselves to share in Christ's redemptive work. But Christian spouses and the families rooted in their conjugal union have, John Paul II insists, a *specific and original role* to play in the drama of redemption. Christ himself has entrusted to the family, the "church in miniature", the specific and indispensable role of building up "the kingdom of God in history *through the everyday realities that concern and distinguish its state of life*. It is thus", he says, "*in the love between husband and wife and between the members of the*

[12] Ibid., no. 13.

[13] Ibid. The internal citation is from John Paul II, Address to the Delegates of the Centre de Liaison des Equipes de Recherche (November 3, 1979), 3; in *Insegnamenti di Giovanni Paolo II*, 2/2 (1979): 1038.

family—a love lived out in all its extraordinary richness of values and demands: totality, oneness, fidelity and fruitfulness—that the Christian family's participation in the prophetic, priestly and kingly mission of Jesus Christ and of his Church finds expression and realization." [14] In short, it is by *realizing itself as such*, and not by any task superimposed on it, that the Christian family acquits its specific and original ecclesial mission. Christian conjugal love, therefore, is the dynamic source of the Christian family's saving mission in the Church and for the Church.

Thus it is important to look more closely at conjugal love as this dynamic source of the Christian family's saving mission before turning attention to its *Christological axis*.

Christian Conjugal Love as the Dynamic Source of the Christian Family's Saving Mission in the Church and for the Church

John Paul II insists that the Christian family builds up the Kingdom of God in history

> through the everyday realities that concern and distinguish its *state of life*. It is thus in *the love between husband and wife and between the members of the family*—a love lived out in all its extraordinary richness of values and demands totality, oneness, fidelity and fruitfulness—that the Christian family's participation in the prophetic, priestly, and kingly mission of Jesus Christ and of his Church finds expression and realization. Therefore, love and life constitute the nucleus of the saving mission of the Christian family in the Church and for the Church. [14]

It is obvious that the love to which John Paul II here refers is the love specific to spouses—and to Christian spouses, for within this passage he explicitly refers to the teaching of Paul VI on the nature of conjugal love in his Encyclical *Humanae vitae* (no. 9), a text in which Paul himself summarized accurately the teaching set forth by Vatican Council II on the nature of this love (cf. *Gaudium et spes*, nos. 49–50). This love is characterized as one that is

[14] Ibid., no. 50.

human, total, faithful and exclusive, and fruitful, and as a love proper and unique to spouses.

Earlier in *Familiaris consortio* John Paul II had emphasized that love is the *inner principle* of the family's life and mission. Indeed, he stressed that "*without love the family cannot live, grow and perfect itself as a community of persons*" (no. 18). He then said: "the love between husband and wife and, in a *derivatory* and broader way, the love between members of the same family—between parents and children, brothers and sisters and relatives and members of the household—is given life and sustenance by an unceasing inner dynamism leading the family to an ever deeper and more intense *communion*, which is the foundation and soul of the *community* of marriage and the family" (no. 18, emphasis in the original). Note that here John Paul II explicitly says that the love between parents and children, brothers and sisters and relatives and household members, *derives* from the love specific to husband and wife, i.e., from *conjugal love*. This is the love that is the life-giving principle of marriage and the inner dynamic principle giving to marriage and the family the capacity to carry out rightly its specific and original ecclesial role.

It is thus crucially important to have a proper understanding of the nature of conjugal love and its place within the structure of marriage. This understanding was beautifully expressed by the teaching of Vatican Council II in *Gaudium et spes*, a teaching wholeheartedly embraced and developed by John Paul II. Many, however, have gravely misinterpreted the teaching of Vatican Council II, claiming that the Council Fathers repudiated the traditional understanding that the procreation and education of children is the primary end of marriage and that it raised conjugal love to the level of an objective *end* of marriage, equal to if not superior to the procreation and education of children.[15] This interpretation of *Gaudium et spes* is, unfortunately, quite widespread today.

---

[15] See, for example, the following: V. Heylin, "La promozione della dignita del matrimonio e della famiglia", in *La Chiesa nel mondo di oggi*, Studi e commenti intorno alla Costituzione pastorale *"Gaudium et spes"* (Florence: Vallacchi, 1966), p. 358; Theodore Mackin, *What Is Marriage?* (New York: Paulist Press, 1982), pp. 235–37, in which he claims that Vatican Council II repudiated the teaching of Pius XII and instead adopted the view of Herbert Doms which had been cen-

A careful study of the conciliar text, however, shows that this is a gravely flawed interpretation.[16] It is true that the Council refused to use the terminology of "primary" and "secondary" ends. But it did so, as the *Acta* of the Council make clear, only because this technical and juridical terminology was judged inappropriate for a document of a pastoral nature. The *Acta* likewise make it clear that the definitive text submitted to the Council Fathers and accepted by them clearly identifies the procreation and the education of children as the primordial end of both the institution of marriage *and* conjugal love.[17]

Conjugal love is *never* described by the Council as an *end* of marriage. Rather, the *end* toward which conjugal love, as indeed the entire institution of marriage, is ordered, is indeed the procreation and education of children (cf. *Gaudium et spes*, nos. 48, 50). The text of *Gaudium et spes* never speaks of conjugal love as an end of marriage; it does not even conceive it as a property of marriage. On the contrary, it consistently predicates of conjugal love the same ends (primordially, the procreation and education of children; subsidiarily, mutual help and assistance) and

---

sured by that pontiff; Michael Lawler, *Secular Marriage, Christian Sacrament* (Mystic, Conn.: Twenty-Third Publications, 1985), p. 53.

[16] In my opinion, the best analysis of the teaching of *Gaudium et spes* on the proper place of conjugal love within the structure of marriage is Gil Hellín's "El lugar propio del amor", *Annales Valentinos* 6 (1980): 1–35. See also Gil Hellín, "El Matrimonio", García de Haro, *Marriage and Family*, pp. 234–56.

[17] See *Acta Synodalia*, Vol. IV, pars VII, p. 472: Under (c) the Council Commission says that "in a *pastoral* text which seeks to establish dialogue with the world these juridical elements ['primary' and 'secondary' ends] are not required." Under (f) the Commission notes that "many documents of tradition and the Magisterium are nonetheless cited [in the text] in which the discourse [*sermo*] concerns these goods and ends". [see footnote 1 of *Gaudium et spes*, no. 48 where reference is made to] St. Augustine, *De bono coniugii*, PL 40:375–76 and 394; Thomas Aquinas, *Summa theologiae*, supplement to part III, q. 49, a. 3 ad 1; *Decretum pro Armenis*: Denz.Schon., 1327; Pius XI, Encyclical *Casti connubii*: AAS 22 (1930): 547–48.... Moreover, the *primordial importance* [*momentum primordiale*] of the procreation and education of children is set forth at least ten times within the text...."

the same properties that they predicate of the whole institution of marriage.

Indeed, according to the thought of Vatican II, conjugal love is the *life-giving* principle of marriage, which the institution of marriage is designed to protect, precisely the same thought set forth by John Paul II in *Familiaris consortio*, no. 11. Conjugal love is indeed what constitutes the personal reality which the institution of marriage confirms, protects, and sanctions before God and man. This is central to the teaching of Vatican Council II, which affirmed that "from the conjugal covenant ... that is, from the human act by which the spouses mutually give and receive each other, there arises in society an institution [marriage], confirmed by divine ordination; this holy bond (*hoc vinculum sacrum*), for the good of the spouses themselves, for the good of their children, and for the good of society, does not depend on upon human choice. God himself is the author of marriage, endowed with various goods and ends" (*Gaudium et spes*, no. 48). What this means is that the institution of marriage comes to be from an act of conjugal love—the act whereby the man and the woman irrevocably give themselves to each other as husband and wife—and the institution protects love, for true conjugal love is not limited or impeded by it, but rather both these elements, the institution of marriage and conjugal love, require and complete each other, as integrative elements of the one same reality: marriage or the conjugal community. As Francisco Gil Hellín has said, conjugal love and the institution of marriage "come to be in a mutual and essential dependence, and they constantly require each other: *love* has need of the institution in order to be conjugal, and the institution of marriage always implies a radical exigency to be enlivened by love." [18] John Paul II confirms this when he says:

> The only "place" in which this self-giving [the self-giving proper to conjugal love] in its whole truth is made possible is marriage, covenant of conjugal love freely and consciously chosen, whereby man and woman accept the intimate community of life and love

[18] Gil Hellín, "El lugar propio del amor conyugal ...", p. 35.

willed by God himself [cf. *Gaudium et spes*, no. 48] ... The institution of marriage is not an undue interference by society or authority.... Rather it is an interior requirement of the covenant of conjugal love. (*Familiaris consortio*, no. 11)

But what is conjugal love? According to the teaching of Vatican Council II conjugal love is not a passion or mere sentiment, but that "eminently human" affection that proceeds from free will and assumes into itself, ennobling them, all the natural tendencies of the person: "That love, as eminently human, since it is directed from one person to another person by an affection rooted in the will, embraces the good of the whole person and therefore is capable of enriching with a peculiar dignity the manifestations of both mind and body and to ennoble them as elements and special signs of conjugal friendship" (*Gaudium et spes*, no. 49). Continuing, in a most important passage, the Council Fathers go on to say that Our Lord has deigned "to heal, perfect, and elevate this love with a special gift of grace and of charity. A love like this, bringing together the human and the divine, leads the spouses to the free and mutual gift of themselves, experienced in tender affection and action, and permeates the whole of their lives [cf. Pius XI, *Casti connubii*: AAS 22 (1930): 547–48]; moreover, this love is perfected and grows by its generous exercise." [19] God's grace, therefore, heals and perfects the nature of conjugal love, establishing marriage as a sacrament and married life as a divine vocation.

Conjugal love is characterized by the properties of unity and indissolubility. Already on the plane of nature—of God the Creator's plan—it has this requirement: "This intimate union, as the mutual giving of two persons, as well as the good of the children, demand the full fidelity of the spouses and require their indissoluble unity" (*Gaudium et spes*, no. 48). And both these properties of conjugal love are confirmed and ratified by grace: "Christ remains with them [the spouses], so that just as he loved the Church and gave himself up for her, so too the spouses, by their mutual self-giving, may love each other with perpetual fidelity" (no. 48). Indeed, "this love, endorsed by mutual fidelity, and above all

[19] *Gaudium et spes*, no. 49.

consecrated by Christ's sacrament, is indissolubly faithful amidst prosperity and adversity of both the body and of the spirit, and consequently remains foreign to every kind of adultery and divorce. The unity of marriage, confirmed by the Lord, shines forth brilliantly in the equal personal dignity which must be given to man and wife in mutual and unreserved love" (no. 49).

And finally, *Gaudium et spes* teaches that *conjugal love has as its intrinsic end the procreation and education of children* (cf. nos. 48, 50). Indeed, the Council insists that "the true cultivation of conjugal love and the whole structure of family life arising therefore, without neglecting the other ends of marriage, tend to this, that the spouses are disposed by a courageous spirit to cooperate with the love of the Creator and Redeemer, who through them will day by day increase and enrich his family" (no. 50). Indeed, one of the most novel affirmations of *Gaudium et spes*, one which marks true theological development on the matter, is that conjugal love, and not only marriage as an institution, has as its end the procreation and education of children.

> What distinguishes the text, in relationship to the previous Magisterium on the ends of marriage, is that it distinguishes between two formally diverse elements contained in the conjugal community [the institution of marriage and conjugal love]. It thus makes explicit "the significance of conjugal love even for the procreating and educating of children".[20]

While up to now the Magisterium of the Church affirmed that marriage "tends toward the procreation and education of children", Vatican Council II tells us that both the institutional aspect and conjugal love "tend toward the procreation and education of children".[21]

Conjugal love, therefore, is regarded by Vatican Council II and by John Paul II as the inner principle of marriage and of the vocation of married couples. Conjugal love is thus essential

[20] *Acta Synodalia*, Vol. IV, pars 1, p. 536, *Relatio ad Schema receptum:* "Mentio fit duo, uti multi patres petierunt, de matrimonio simul et amore. Momentum etiam amoris coniugalis etiam ad ipsam procreandam educandamque sublineatur."

[21] Gil Hellín, "El lugar propio del amor conyugal", p. 16.

to marriage. This does not, however, mean that, should conjugal love "die", the marriage dies.[22] As we have seen, the first act of conjugal love is the act of irrevocable personal consent whereby the man and the woman unconditionally and irrevocably give themselves to each other as husband and wife. Conjugal love is included in the object of their consent, as the Christian tradition has consistently taught.[23] In the conjugal community, conjugal love is the life-giving principle owed by virtue of the very consent that has generated it. Nonetheless, its absence from a marriage does not destroy it. This is so because marriage, while born from the human act that brings it into being, does not depend upon their arbitrary will (cf. *Gaudium et spes*, no. 48). Therefore, the unjust and unlawful violation later on of the requirements of love cannot annul either the consent nor the community, as Vatican Council II insisted.[24] Within the conjugal community conjugal love is an essential good, existing at least as a *requirement*. Moreover, for Christian spouses, there is the assurance that God and Christ, who led them *to* marriage, are with them *in* marriage, ever ready to enable them to give one another the conjugal love that is the life-giving principle and of the mission that has been entrusted to them. This love finds its fulfillment in the mutual sanctification of the spouses, a sanctification that requires them to carry out rightly the three-fold mission that has been entrusted to them, the mission to which I shall now turn.

And this is a fitting way to introduce the *christological* axis of the domestic church.

---

[22] This, unfortunately, is the claim of some contemporary theologians. See, for instant, Mackin, *What Is Marriage?*, p. 315, where he writes: "Since, according to *Gaudium et spes*, a marriage is to be understood as an intimate community of life and marital love, it can dissolve and disintegrate."

[23] See, for instance, St. Augustine, *De bono coniugali*, cap. 3, n. 3; PL 40:375; Thomas Aquinas, *Summa theologiae*, supplement to part III, q. 49, a. 3.

[24] See *Gaudium et spes*, no. 48. *Acta Synodalia*, vol. IV, pars I, p. 536: *Relatio ad Schema receptum*: "Notio instituti matrimonii sequenti phrasi firmatur, ne ullus censeat sese illud arbitrio suo postea dissolver posse; aut, deficiente amore etiam requisito, matrimonium suum nullum fieri."

The Christological Axis

This axis was not ignored in presenting the ecclesial axis of the family as domestic church, insofar as Christ is inseparable from his body, the Church. John Paul II, however, explicitly develops the *christological* axis when he affirms that to understand the "substance" of the family we must always do so "in reference to Jesus Christ as Prophet, Priest and King" (*Familiaris consortio*, no. 51).

As far as the substantive content of this mission is concerned, John Paul II uses the scheme of participation in the threefold mission of Christ as Prophet, Priest, and King and thus presents the Christian family under the threefold aspect of being a believing and evangelizing community, a community in dialogue with God, and a community at the service of mankind.

The family as a believing and evangelizing community: its prophetic role. The Christian family shares in Christ's prophetic mission "by welcoming and announcing the word of God".[25] Thus the first requirement of Christian spouses and parents is faith, because "only in faith can they discover and admire with joyful gratitude the dignity to which God has deigned to raise marriage and the family, making them a sign and meeting place of the loving covenant between God and man, between Jesus Christ and his bride, the Church" (no. 51). The driving force of the Christian family is, as we will see, the love specific to spouses, but Christian spouses know through faith that their love is a sign and real participation in the love of God and in his redemptive power. God, who through faith "called the couple *to* marriage, continues to call them *in* marriage. In and through the events, problems, difficulties, and circumstances of everyday life, God comes to them, revealing and presenting the concrete 'demands' of their sharing in the love of Christ for his Church in the particular family, social, and ecclesial situation in which they find themselves." [26]

[25] *Familiares consortio*, no. 51.
[26] Ibid. Here John Paul II explicitly refers to what Paul VI had taught in *Humanae vitae*, no. 25.

Faith thus heard and experienced in love makes the Christian family a fire that sheds its light on many other families (cf. no. 52). This prophetic mission of the family, John Paul II emphasizes, is the dynamic expression of its inner identity; the family carries this mission out by being faithful to its own proper being as a community of life and love: "[the] apostolic mission of the family is rooted in baptism and receives from the grace of the sacrament of marriage new strength to transmit the faith, to sanctify and transform our present society according to God's plan." [27]

The pope notes two characteristics of the prophetic apostolate of the family. First of all, it is exercised within the family itself by encouraging and helping family members to live fully their Christian vocation. Wisely, the Holy Father notes that "just as in the Church the work of evangelization can never be separated from the sufferings of the apostle, so in the Christian family parents must face with courage and great interior serenity the difficulties that their ministry of evangelization sometimes encounters in their own children." [28] In addition, this prophetic and evangelizing apostolate, begun within the family itself, includes the "task of defending and spreading the faith, a task that has its roots in baptism and confirmation, and makes Christian married couples and parents witnesses of Christ 'to the ends of the earth,' missionaries, in the true and proper sense, of love and life". [29] One form of this missionary activity, John Paul II observes, "can be exercised even within the family. This happens when some member of the family does not have the faith or does not practice it with consistency. In such a case the other members must give him or her a living witness of their own faith in order to encourage and support him or her along the path towards full acceptance of Christ the Savior." [30]

---

[27] Ibid., no. 52.
[28] Ibid., no. 53.
[29] Ibid., no. 54.
[30] Ibid.

The family as a community in dialogue with God: its priestly role. John
Paul II begins his presentation of this essential task of the Christian family by reminding us that marriage is a sacrament of mutual
sanctification and of worship and that the love of Christian spouses
has been judged by the Lord, as Vatican Council II had noted
earlier, "worthy of special gifts, healing, perfecting and exalting
gifts of grace and of charity".[31] Moreover, "the gift of Jesus Christ
is not exhausted in the actual celebration of the sacrament of
marriage, but rather accompanies the married couple throughout
their lives."[32]

Precisely because Christian marriage is a sacrament of mutual
sanctification, the universal call of all Christians to holiness is,
for Christian spouses and parents, "specified by the sacrament
they have celebrated and is carried out concretely in the realities
proper to their conjugal and family life".[33] John Paul II then
emphasizes the *sacramental foundation* of the sanctity demanded of
spouses. Holiness is not easy, and it lies beyond merely human
powers. To sanctify themselves, their children, and the world in
which they live, Christian spouses must have recourse to the
sources of divine grace, in particular the Eucharist and confes-
sion. Just as love is the proper power of the family and participation in Christ's love is what defines the Christian family, so
the Eucharist is the living fountain of Christian married and
family life: "The Eucharist is the very source of Christian marriage. The Eucharistic Sacrifice, in fact, represents Christ's covenant of love with the Church, sealed by his blood on the cross. . . .
[T]he Eucharist is a fountain of charity. In the Eucharistic gift
of charity the Christian family finds the foundation and soul of
its 'communion' and its 'mission'."[34] In addition, it is through
the sacrament of penance that "the married couple and the other
members of the family are led to an encounter with God, who
is 'rich in mercy,' who bestows on them his love which is more

---

[31] Ibid., no. 56. The internal citation is taken from *Gaudium et spes*, no. 49.
[32] Ibid.
[33] Ibid.
[34] Ibid., no. 57.

powerful than sin, and who reconstructs and brings to perfection the marriage covenant and the family communion." [35]

By keeping close to Christ through the sacraments of the Eucharist and of penance and by prayer the Christian family can discover family life itself, in all its circumstances, "as a call from God and as a filial response to his call. Joys and sorrows, hopes and disappointments, births and birthday celebrations, wedding anniversaries of the parents, departures, separations and homecomings, important and far-reaching decisions, the death of those who are dear, etc.—all of these mark God's loving intervention in the family's history. They should be seen as suitable moments for thanksgiving, for petition, for trusting abandonment of the family into the hands of their common Father in heaven." [36]

The family as a community at the service of mankind: its kingly mission. The Christian family exercises this mission by putting itself at the service of others, as Christ did and as he asks his disciples to do.[37] Here the Holy Father stresses that "the law of Christian life is to be found not in a written code but in the personal action of the Holy Spirit who inspires and guides the Christian." For Christian spouses and their families the guide and rule of life is the Spirit of Jesus, the evangelical law of love. Thus, "inspired and sustained by the new commandment of love, the Christian family welcomes, respects, and serves every human being, considering each one in his or her dignity as a person and a child of God." [38] This profound respect for the dignity of human persons must be shown first of all within the family itself—between husband and wife and their children, "through a daily effort to promote a truly personal community, initiated and fostered by an inner communion of love. This way of life should then be extended to the wider circle of the ecclesial community of which the Christian family is a part.... [and ultimately this] love goes beyond our

[35] Ibid., no. 58.
[36] Ibid., no. 59.
[37] Ibid., no. 63.
[38] Ibid., no. 64.

brothers and sisters of the same faith since 'everybody is my brother
or sister.' In each individual, especially in the poor, the weak,
and those who suffer or are unjustly treated, love knows how to
discover the face of Christ and to discover a fellow human being
to be loved and served." [39]

[39] Ibid.

6

John Paul II's Catechesis on the Theology of the Body

Here my purpose is to present key teachings set forth by Pope John Paul II in his catechesis on the Theology of the Body (TOB). But first it seems advisable to say something about TOB, its purpose and argument.

Purpose and Argument of TOB

John Paul's catechesis on the body began on September 5, 1979, and after various interruptions, including the 1981 assassination attempt, ended over five years later on November 28, 1984. The length of this catechesis and its place as John Paul II's first teaching project as pope show its fundamental significance. Thanks to the research of Michael Waldstein, we now know that Karol Wojtyla had written the TOB to be published as a book entitled *Man and Woman He Created Them.*[1] Its publication was interrupted by

[1] On this see Waldstein's Introduction to John Paul II, *Man and Woman He Created Them: A Theology of the Body*, Introduction, Translation, and Index by Michael Waldstein (Boston: Pauline Books and Media, 2006), pp. 7–11. All translations of TOB will be taken from this source. References will be made to the number of the Audience (133 are given in the new translation), the paragraph number of that Audience, and the page on which it appears in the new translation. Thus *Man and Woman* 4.3, p. 143 refers to Audience 4, paragraph no. 3, page 143 of the Waldstein translation.

Also see the commentary on John Paul II's Theology of the Body by Christopher West, *Theology of the Body Explained: A Commentary on John Paul II's Man*

Wojtyla's election as pope on October 16, 1978. Providentially, however, this gave the text another destiny and a much wider audience. It also made it an official work of John Paul II's Magisterium, rather than the private work of a Polish theologian. Sometime after his election, John Paul II personally adapted his manuscript for the Wednesday Audience format.

In his excellent Introduction to his new and accurate translation of TOB, Waldstein shows that TOB has a twofold purpose: to defend (1) the reality of the human body and (2) Pope Paul VI's Encyclical *Humanae vitae*. Waldstein demonstrates that TOB gathers up the dominant concerns of Wojtyla/John Paul II's earlier philosophical and theological work, grouping them into three phases, the *beginning*, the *challenge*, and the *response*. Its *beginning* is found in Wojtyla's rooting of his personalism in that of St. John of the Cross and his development of this personalism during his experience of Vatican II and in working out TOB. The *challenge* is posed by the new understanding of human subjectivity and "personalism" based on Bacon and Descartes, developed by Kant, and central to the essentialist phenomenology of Scheler. This new "personalism" regards the human body as mere matter, part of the subpersonal world over which the "subject/person" has dominion and as such is itself not personal.[2] The *response* is the pope's defense of the body as integral to the *being* of the human person.

John Paul II himself shows that TOB is a defense of *Humanae vitae* in particular in the very last Wednesday Audience (*Man and Woman* 133). There, as Waldstein notes, John Paul "points to the encyclical *Humanae Vitae* as the true focus of TOB as a whole" (*Man and Woman*, p. 99). Thus the Holy Father declared in that address:

> The catecheses devoted to *Humanae Vitae* constitute only one small part, the final part, of those that dealt with the redemption of the body and the sacramentality of marriage.

---

and Woman He Created Them, with an Introduction by Michael Waldstein (Boston: Pauline Books and Media, 2007), a revision of his earlier book on this subject.

[2] Ibid., pp. 94–95.

If I draw particular attention to these final catecheses, I do so not only because the topic discussed by them is more closely connected with our present age, but first of all because *it is from this topic that the questions spring* that run in some way through the whole of our reflections. It follows that this final part is not artificially added to the whole, but is organically and homogeneously united with it. In some sense, that part, which in the overall disposition is located at the end, is at the same time found at the beginning of that whole. This is important from the point of view of structure and method. (133.4, p. 662; all emphasis in the text, unless noted, is in the original) [3]

In his catechis on the TOB, John Paul II took pains to show that the anthropology underlying the defense of contraception mounted by the authors of the celebrated "Majority Report" of the Papal Commission on the regulation of birth (released to the press in 1967) is the same as the dualistic anthropology at the heart of the Cartesian-Kantian-Schelerian divorce of the "person" from the body.[4] To defend the encyclical and to provide the needed "integral vision" called for by Paul VI, John Paul II in *Man and Woman* offered a "rereading of the 'theology of the body' in the 'truth'", i.e., in the light of Christ's incarnation and revelation of man to man himself.

Waldstein follows the text as divided and entitled by the Holy Father himself because, as the John Paul Archives on which Waldstein's new translation is based clearly show, this is John Paul II's own way of *structuring* the text and its *argument*. The overall structure of *Man and Woman* can be seen by the titles Karol Wojtyla/John Paul II assigned to its major divisions.

Part 1. The Words of Christ
Chapter 1: Christ Appeals to the "Beginning" (1–23); Chapter 2: Christ Appeals to the Human Heart (24–63); Chapter 3: Christ Appeals to the Resurrection (64–86) [Conclusion of Part 1: The Redemption of the Body].

Part 2. The Sacrament
Chapter 1: The Dimension of Covenant and of Grace (87–102); Chapter 2: The Dimension of Sign (103–17); Chapter 3: He Gave Them the Law of Life as Their Inheritance (118–32); [Conclusion: 133].

[3] See ibid., pp. 99–100.
[4] Ibid., pp. 100–3.

The titles John Paul II gave to the whole show us how the first two parts ("The Words of Christ" and "The Sacrament") are interrelated and serve the overall purpose of *Man and Woman*. This is evident from a significant passage from the final address in which John Paul II declared, "The whole of the catecheses that I began more than four years ago and that I conclude today can be grasped under the title, 'Human Love in the Divine Plan,' or with greater precision, 'The Redemption of the Body and the Sacramentality of Marriage'" (133.1, p. 659). Commenting on this passage, Waldstein says:

> The overall title mentions a single subject, "Human Love in the Divine Plan," while the subtitle has two parts, "The Redemption of the Body" and "The Sacramentality of Marriage." Since John Paul II says in the text quoted above that Part 2 is about "the sacramentality of marriage," one is led to assume that Part 1 is about "the redemption of the body." The Conclusion of Part 1 (TOB 86) confirms this assumption. It focuses on "the redemption of the body." At the very end of that Conclusion, John Paul II writes, "Everything we have tried to do in the course of our meditations in order to understand the words of Christ has its definitive foundation in the mystery of the redemption of the body" (TOB 86:8). (*Man and Woman*, p. 110)

In John Paul's *Man and Woman* the redemption of the body is the end that determines all steps. In many ways Part 1 ("The Words of Christ") itself offers a Theology of the Body. "Since the 'redemption of the body' is the final end considered by a theology of the body," Waldstein writes, "reflection on it implies a complete theology of the body in all its essential articulations" (pp. 110–11). He then cites an important passage from *Man and Woman* in which John Paul II declares:

> To understand all that "the redemption of the body" implies according to Romans, an authentic theology of the body is necessary. We have attempted to build one, appealing first of all to the words of Christ. The constitutive elements of the theology of the body are contained in what Christ says when he appeals to the "beginning" concerning the question of the indissolubility of marriage

(see Mt 19:8), in what he says about concupiscence when he appeals to the human heart in the Sermon on the Mount (see Mt 5:28), and also in what he says when he appeals to the resurrection (see Mt 22:30). Each one of these statements contains in itself a rich content of an anthropological as well as ethical nature. Christ speaks to man—and speaks about man, who is a "body" and is created as male and female in the image and likeness of God; he speaks about man, whose heart is subjected to concupiscence; and, finally, about man, before whom the eschatological perspective of the resurrection of the body opens up. (86.4, pp. 460–70)

"This text is helpful", Waldstein writes, "for understanding the function of Part 1. When it analyzes the three words of Jesus from the point of view of 'the redemption of the body,' Part 1 presents all 'the constitutive elements of the theology of the body'" (p. 111).

Part 2 then deepens and unfolds Part 1; in it John Paul II argues that the redemption of the body is definitively accomplished in the final and glorious realization of the spousal meaning of the body in the resurrection and beatific vision (67–68). From the very "beginning," the spousal meaning of the body in the love between man and woman is a sign that manifests and communicates holiness (19.3–6), signifying the covenant between God and his people, between Christ and the Church, and ultimately the mystery of the communion among the divine persons in the Trinity. Thus, after providing in Part 1 a comprehensive account of the redemption, John Paul II deepens and unfolds this account in Part 2 "by focusing on the '*sacramentum magnum*,' the great mystery of love revealed in Ephesians 5" (pp. 110–12). Thus, Waldstein concludes, the *argument* of *Man and Woman* can be summarized thus:

> The main argument of TOB is … very simple and clear. Its first step consists in unfolding the teaching of Jesus about the spousal meaning of the body (in its three dimensions: in God's original plan "from the beginning"; in the present struggle with concupiscence; and in the future fulfillment by the resurrection). Its second step consists in observing how this spousal meaning functions in the great sacrament of love, particularly in the language

of the body that is the effective sign of this sacrament. Its third step consists in showing that *Humanae Vitae* simply asks men and women to reread this language of the body in the truth. The persuasive power of the argument lies in its ability to bring the teaching of Jesus to bear on the question of the genuine development and happiness of the human person. Jesus' teaching has an *inner* persuasive power, which lies in the beauty of God's plan for human love. (p. 124)

I use this final citation from Waldstein to organize this chapter. Thus I first present at some length John Paul II's teaching about the spousal meaning of the body in God's original plan in the beginning, in the present struggle with concupiscence, and its future fulfillment in the resurrection. I then more briefly show how spousal love functions in the sacrament of marriage and the language of the body. I will conclude by taking up the relationship between the language of the body and the teaching of *Humanae vitae*.

Marriage and the Spousal Meaning of the Body in God's Original Plan, in the Present Struggle with Concupiscence, and in Its Future Fulfillment in the Resurrection

1. In God's Original Plan

John Paul II begins his catechesis on the Theology of the Body by taking as his starting point Christ's reply to the question raised by the Pharisees, "Is it lawful for a man to divorce his wife for any reason?"—namely, "Have you not read that from the beginning *the Creator created them male and female?* and said '*For this reason a man will leave his father and his mother and unite with his wife and the two will be one flesh?*' ... Therefore what God has joined let man not separate" (Mt 19:3–6). Since Christ quoted Genesis in his reply, John Paul II says we must return to the "beginning" to discover God's loving plan for human persons, male and female. Christ makes it clear that "Genesis 2:24 states the principle of the unity and indissolubility of marriage as the very content of the word of God expressed in the most ancient revelation" (1.3, p. 132). The "significant expression: 'from the beginning,' repeated twice, clearly leads the interlocutors to reflect about the way in which, in the mystery of creation, man was formed precisely as 'male and female,' in order to understand correctly the normative meaning of the words of Genesis" (1.4, p. 133).

In his analyses of the "creation accounts" in Genesis 1 (attributed to the Elohist source) and Genesis 2 (attributed to the Yahwist source) John Paul II emphasizes that the human body reveals the human person and has a "spousal" meaning. The Holy Father introduces the first truth—that the human body reveals the human person—in commenting on Genesis 2:18, which speaks of the man being "alone". He emphasizes that here the issue is the solitude of "'man' (male and female) and not only with the solitude of the man-male, caused by the absence of the woman. . . . [T]his *solitude has two meanings: one deriving from man's very nature*, that is, from his humanity . . . and *the other deriving from the relationship between male and female*" (5.2, p. 147). The solitude deriving from man's very nature, John Paul II says, enables us "to *link man's original solitude with the awareness of the body*, through which man distinguishes himself from all the *animalia* and 'separates himself' from them, and *through which* he is a *person*. One can affirm with certainty that the man thus formed has at the same time consciousness and awareness of the meaning of his own body. Moreover, [he has] this based on the experience of original solitude" (6.3, p. 152).

In short, man's awareness of his body as different from the bodies of other animals enables him to grasp the truth that he, alone among visible creatures, is a *person*, gifted with self-consciousness and self-determination.

The Holy Father perhaps most dramatically shows that the human body reveals the human person and in doing so also reveals the spousal meaning of the body when he considers the second meaning of man's "solitude" and reflects on the text of Genesis 2:18–24, which describes in poetic terms the "creation" of woman. "When the first man exclaims at the sight of the woman, 'she is flesh from my flesh and bone from my bones' (Gen 2:23), he simply affirms", the pope says, "the human identity of both. By exclaiming this, he seems to say, '*Look, a body that expresses the "person"!*'" (14.4, p. 183).

Since the body expresses the person, and since persons are to be loved, an ethical consequence is that we must never express with our bodies anything unworthy of the person. The body is a beautiful manifestation of a human person in all his or her God-given dignity.

John Paul most beautifully shows that the mystery of human nakedness reveals the "spousal meaning of the body". Reflecting once again on the first man's cry of joy, "she is flesh from my flesh and bone from my bones" (Gen 2:23), the pope declares: "these words in some way express the subjectively beatifying beginning of man's existence in the world" (14:3, p. 182). "This beatifying 'beginning' of man's being and existing as male and female", John Paul II continues,

> is connected with the revelation and the discovery of the meaning of the body that is rightly called "spousal."... We have already observed that after the words expressing the first joy of man's coming into existence as "male and female" (Gen 2:23) there follows the verse that establishes their conjugal unity (Gen 2:24), and then the one that attests the nakedness of both without reciprocal shame (Gen 2:25). That these verses face each other in such a significant way allows us to speak *of revelation together with the discovery of the "spousal" meaning of the body in the mystery of creation.* (14.5, p. 183–84)

In short, the male person's body is a sign of the gift of the male person to the female person and vice versa. Because of the spousal meaning of the body, man—male and female—realizes that he can fulfill himself as a person only by giving himself to another in love, in the sincere gift of self. He realizes that his vocation is to love.

In a very beautiful passage John Paul II had this to say:

> While in the mystery of creation the woman is the one who is "given" to the man, he on his part, in receiving her as a gift in the full truth of her person and femininity, enriches her by this very reception, and, at the same time, he too is enriched in this

reciprocal relationship. The man is enriched not only through her, who gives her own person and femininity to him, but also by the gift of self. The man's act of self-donation, in answer to that of the woman, is for him himself an enrichment; in fact, it is here that *the specific essence*, as it were, *of his masculinity is manifested, which, through the reality of the body and of its sex, reaches the innermost depth of "self-possession,"* thanks to which he is able both to give himself and to receive the gift of the other. The man, therefore, not only accepts the gift, but at the same time is welcomed as a gift by the woman in the self-revelation of the inner spiritual essence of his masculinity together with the whole truth of his body and his sex. When he is accepted in this way, he is enriched by this acceptance and welcoming of his own masculinity. It follows that such an acceptance, in which the man finds himself through the "sincere gift of self," becomes in him a source of a new and more profound enrichment of the woman with himself. The exchange is reciprocal, and the mutual effects of the "sincere gift" and of "finding oneself" reveal themselves and grow in that exchange [*Gaudium et Spes*, 24:3]. (17.6, p. 197)

As this text shows, husbands and wives are meant to "give" and "receive" one another precisely in and through the spousal meaning of their bodies. This meaning reflects their sexual complementarity. It seems to me that John Paul's way of articulating the "giving" and "receiving" ("acceptance" is the term used in the text) has been well expressed by Robert Joyce who says that both the man and the woman are to give and to receive in a loving way, but that the man is so constituted in his masculinity that he is emphatically inclined to "give in a receiving sort of way", whereas the woman is so constituted in her femininity that she is emphatically inclined to "receive in a giving sort of way".[5] Indeed, as John Paul II says, it is in the male's "self-oblation" (= giving himself) "that *the specific essence*, as it were, *of his masculinity is manifested, which, through the reality of the body and of its sex, reaches the innermost depth of 'self-possession,'* thanks to which

[5] Robert Joyce, *Human Sexual Ecology: A Philosophy and Ethics of Man and Woman* (Washington, D.C., University Press of America, 1980), pp. 70 ff. See also Chapter Two above.

he is able both to give himself and to receive the gift of the other
... [and] is welcomed [= received] as a gift by the woman."

In a further memorable passage, in which he links the original
spousal meaning of the body to the absence of shame in the state
of original innocence prior to the "fall" (see Gen 2:25), John
Paul then says:

> Happiness is being rooted in Love. Original happiness speaks to
> us about the "beginning" of man, who emerged from love and
> initiated love. And this happened irrevocably, despite the sub-
> sequent sin and death. In his time, Christ was to be a witness to
> this irreversible love of the Creator and Father, which had already
> expressed itself in the mystery of creation and in the grace of
> original innocence. For this reason, also the common "begin-
> ning" of man and woman, that is, the original truth of their body
> in masculinity and femininity, to which Genesis 2:25 turns our
> attention, does not know shame. One can define this "begin-
> ning" also as the original and beatifying immunity from shame as
> the result of love. (16:2; pp. 190–91)

This immunity from shame directs us to the mystery of man's original innocence, which is the mystery of his existence prior to the
knowledge of good and evil and almost "outside" it. The fact that
man exists in this way, before the breaking of the first covenant
with his Creator, belongs to the fullness of the mystery of creation. Why is this so? John Paul II explains it as follows: "If ...
creation is a gift given to man ... then *its fullness* and deepest
dimension is *determined by grace*, that is, by participation in the inner
life of God himself, in his holiness. In man, this holiness is also the
inner foundation and source of his original innocence. With this
concept—and more precisely with that of 'original justice'—
theology defines the state of man before original sin (16.3, p. 191)."

Of crucial importance is the fact that it is "this consciousness
of the body—or even better, *consciousness of the meaning of the body
...* [that] *reveals the distinctive character of original innocence*" (16.3,
p. 191). In fact,

> the body itself of each is a witness of this characteristic, in some
> way an "eyewitness." It is significant that the statement contained

in Genesis 2:25—about reciprocal nakedness free from shame—is a statement unique in its kind in the whole Bible, so much so that it was never to be repeated. On the contrary, we can quote many texts in which nakedness is linked with shame or even, in a still stronger sense, with "defilement" (16.3, pp. 191–92. In footnote 1 John Paul II refers to Hosea 1:2 and Ezekiel 23:26, 29 as texts to illustrate this.)

Original innocence is "that which 'radically,' that is, *at its very roots, excludes the shame of the body* in the relation between man and woman, that which *eliminates the necessity of this shame in man*, in his *heart* or his *consciousness*" and it refers above all to "the interior state of the human 'heart,' of the human 'will'" (16.4, p. 193).

But, and this is most important, in his fourth audience on the Theology of the Body John Paul II insists that the "beginning" to which Christ referred indicated not only man's creation but must be seen within the perspective of the "redemption of the body". In a remarkable text he writes,

> Already in the context of the same Yahwist text of Genesis 2 and 3, we witness the moment in which man, male and female, after having broken the original covenant with his Creator, receives the first promise of redemption in the words of the so-called Proto-evangelium ... and begins to live *in the theological perspective of redemption*. Thus "historical" man ... participates not only *in the history of human sinfulness* ... but he also participates *in the history of salvation*. ... He is ... open to the mystery of the redemption realized in Christ and through Christ. Paul ... expresses this perspective of redemption, in which "historical" man lives, when he writes, "We ourselves, who have the first fruits of the Spirit, groan inwardly while we wait for ... the redemption of our bodies" (Rom 8:23). ... If that "beginning" indicated only the creation of man as "male and female," if ... Christ only led his interlocutors across the boundary of man's state of sin to original innocence and did not open at the same time the perspective of a "redemption of the body," his answer would not at all be understood adequately. Precisely this *perspective of the redemption of the body guarantees the continuity and the unity* between man's hereditary state of sin and his original innocence, although within history this innocence has been irremediably lost by him. (4.3, pp. 143–44)

2. In the Present Struggle with Concupiscence

A key idea in *Man and Woman* is that concupiscence "obscures" the spousal meaning of the body. The pope develops this idea both in his reflections on the third chapter of Genesis, which tells us of the sin of the first man and its dreadful consequences for human existence, and on the teaching in the New Testament on "concupiscence". In reflecting on the Genesis text he likewise highlights the contrast between the lack of shame over their nakedness experienced by Adam and Eve in the state of original innocence and on the shame over their nakedness that they experience after their fall from grace.

Commenting on Genesis 3, John Paul II writes: "The man who picks the fruit of the tree of the knowledge of good and evil makes ... a fundamental choice and carries it through against the will of the Creator, God-Yahweh. ... Man turns his back on God-Love, on the 'Father.'. . . He detaches his heart and cuts it off, as it were, from that which 'comes from the Father': in this way, what is left in him is what 'comes from the world'" (26.4, pp. 236–37). "Then the eyes of both were opened, and they realized that they were naked" (Gen 3:6). Genesis 3.6 speaks explicitly about the birth of shame in connection with sin. That shame is, as it were, the first source of the manifestation in man—in both the man and the woman—of what 'does not come from the Father, but from the world'" (26.5, p. 237–38).

Because of their shame man and woman find it necessary to hide from God. "The need to hide shows that, *in the depth of the shame they feel before each other* as the immediate fruit of the tree of the knowledge of good and evil, *a sense of fear before God has matured: a fear previously unknown*" (27.1, p. 238). John Paul II continues:

> A certain fear is always part of the very essence of shame; nevertheless, original shame reveals its character in a particular way. "I was afraid, because I am naked." We realize that something deeper is at stake here than mere bodily shame. ... With his shame about his own nakedness, the man seeks to cover the true origin of fear by indicating the effect so as not to name the cause. ...

In reality, what shows itself through "nakedness" is man deprived of participation in the Gift, man alienated from the Love that was the source of the original gift, the source of the fullness of good intended for the creature. This man, according to the formulas of the Church's theological teaching, was deprived of the supernatural and preternatural gifts that were part of his "endowment" before sin; in addition, he suffered damage in what belongs to nature itself, to humanity in the original fullness "of the image of God." (27.1–2, pp. 239–40; emphasis added)

Shame is the sign that a radical change has come over man. In the state of original innocence nakedness did not express a lack but rather a full acceptance of the body in all its human and personal truth. It was "a faithful witness and a perceptible verification of man's original 'solitude' in the world, while becoming at the same time, through masculinity and femininity, a transparent component of reciprocal giving in the communion of persons" (27.3, p. 241). But now, as a result of original sin and of the concupiscence that has entered his "heart", man has lost, in a way, *the original certainty of the 'image of God' expressed in his body*" (27.4, p. 241). This, John Paul II says, can be called the "cosmic shame" that man experienced with regard to his Creator.

This "cosmic shame" makes way in the biblical text for another form of shame—"the shame produced in humanity itself", an "immanent and relative" shame:

This is the shame of woman "with regard to" man, and also of man "with regard to" woman: a reciprocal shame.... The Yahwist text seems to indicate explicitly the "sexual" character of this shame. "They sewed fig leaves together and made themselves loinclothes." Nevertheless, we can ask ourselves whether the "sexual" aspect has only a "relative" character; in other words, whether it is a question of shame of one's own sexuality only in reference to the person of the other sex. (28.1, p. 243)

The pope then clarifies the "immanent" and "relative" meanings of sexual shame. He maintains that although the text of Genesis 3:7 ("the eyes of both of them were opened . . .") seems to support the relative character of original shame; nonetheless deeper reflection

> allows us to discover its more immanent background. That shame, which shows itself without any doubt in the "sexual" order, reveals *a specific difficulty in sensing the human essentiality of one's own body*, a difficulty man had not experienced in the state of original innocence. In this way, in fact, one can understand the words, "I was afraid because I am naked." ... These words reveal a certain constitutive fracture in the human person's interior, *a breakup, as it were, of man's original spiritual and somatic unity*. (28.2, pp. 243–44)

Immanent shame, the pope writes,

> contains such a cognitive sharpness that it creates a fundamental disquiet in the whole of human existence.... *The body is not subject to the spirit as in the state of original innocence, but carries within itself a constant hotbed of resistance to the spirit and threatens in some way man's unity as a person, that is, the unity of the moral nature that plunges its roots firmly into the very constitution of the person. The concupiscence of the body is a specific threat to the structure of self-possession and self-dominion, through which the human person forms itself.* (28.3, p. 244; emphasis added)

Shame has a double meaning: "it indicates the threat to the value and at the same time it preserves this value in an interior way" (28.6, p. 246). Shame is experienced because one fears that the sexual values of his body will be consumed by the lust of others and he thus seeks to protect those values because they are *personal*.

Turning his attention to the subject of concupiscence, the Holy Father shows how it menaces the "communion of persons" and distorts the spousal meaning of the body. Since the body, after the fall, no longer expresses the person adequately, "the original power of communicating themselves to each other, about which Genesis 2:25 speaks, has been shattered" (29.2, p. 247). Because of concupiscence the man will want to "dominate" the woman and the woman, who will desire her husband (cf. Gen 3:16), will feel a lack of full unity. Thus the "*original beatifying conjugal union of persons was to be deformed in man's heart by concupiscence*" (30.4, p. 251). An adequate analysis of Genesis 3, he maintains, "leads thus to the conclusion that the threefold concupiscence [referred to in Jn 2:16–17], including that of the body, brings with it a limitation of the spousal meaning of the body itself, the spousal meaning in which man and woman shared in the state of original innocence" (31.5, p. 255). Nonetheless, the human body, independently of our states of consciousness and our experiences, retains its spousal meaning (cf. 30.5).

In the Sermon on the Mount Jesus deepens the meaning of the commandment "Do not commit adultery" by revealing the ethical meaning of the commandment (36.1, p. 271). Christ speaks of "adultery in the heart". If the fundamental meaning of adultery is that of a sin of the body, how can what a man does in his heart also count as adultery? "The man about whom Christ speaks in the Sermon on the Mount—the man who looks 'to desire'—is without doubt the man of concupiscence" (38.2, p. 279). But to see why he must be regarded as committing adultery we must recognize the ethical and anthropological significance of the "look to desire" or "lustful look".

"*The look*", the Holy Father says, "*expresses what is in the heart.* The look, I would say, expresses man as a whole. If one assumes that man in general 'acts in conformity with what he is' (*operari sequitur esse* [operation follows being]), in the present case Christ wants to show that man 'looks' in conformity with what he is: *intueri sequitur esse* [looking follows being]" (39.4, p. 285). Continuing, the pope says:

> "looking to desire" indicates an experience of the value of the body in which its spousal meaning ceases to be spousal precisely because of concupiscence. What also ceases is its procreative meaning. . . . So then, when man "desires" and "looks to desire" . . . he *experiences* more or less explicitly *the detachment from that meaning of the body* which . . . stands at the basis of the communion of persons: both outside of marriage and—in a particular way—when man and woman are called to build their union "in the body". (39.5, pp. 285–86)

In further analyzing concupiscent desire, John Paul characterizes it as deceiving the human heart with respect to the perennial call to man and woman to "give" themselves and establish a communion of persons, a call revealed in the mystery of creation and mediated by the body. Thus concupiscent "desire as a realization of the concupiscence of the flesh ... diminishes the meaning of ... this invitation" (40.2, p. 287). Concupiscent desire is thus, he continues, "an *intentional 'reduction,'* a restriction, as it were, or closure of the horizon of the mind and the heart". It leads one to ignore the value of the person as person, a being to be loved, and focuses on the person's *sexual values* as the only real values and "fitting object of the satisfaction of one's own sexuality" (40.3, pp. 287 and 288).

From this it follows that although society does not regard the exterior act of genital union between a married man and his own wife as "adultery" (42.5, p. 295),

> we conclude that ... in *understanding* "adultery in the heart," Christ takes into consideration not only the real juridical state of life of the man and the woman in question. Christ makes the moral evaluation of "desire" *depend above all on the personal dignity of the man and the woman*; and this is important both in the case of unmarried persons and—perhaps even more so—in the case of spouses, husband and wife. (42.7, p. 297; emphasis added; see 43.1)

The Holy Father then concludes: "Adultery 'in the heart' is not committed only because man 'looks' in this way at a woman who is not his wife, but *precisely because he looks in this way at a woman. Even* if he were to look in this way at the woman who is his wife, he would commit the same adultery 'in the heart'" (43.2, p. 298).

Since Pope John Paul II's teaching here evoked outrage in some persons[6] it is important that in speaking in this way he not only reaffirmed the teaching of Church Fathers such as St. Augustine and of St. Thomas Aquinas but even more importantly articulated a great truth of which people today need to be reminded. Today in our culture there is much talk of "spousal abuse", and it is surely true that a married man, for example, may seek genital

---

[6] See *L'Osservatore Romano*, October 12, 1980; West, *Theology of the Body Explained*, p. 235.

sex with his spouse not as a means of expressing his love for her but solely as a means to gratify his sexual desires here and now and uses her body for this purpose.

3. In Its Future Fulfillment in the Resurrection

Another concept central to *Man and Woman* is that by union with Christ man can rediscover the spousal meaning of the body. He can do so because Christ has won for us the *redemption of the body*. The Pope develops this idea in his reflections on our Lord's Sermon on the Mount (Mt 5) and on the teaching of St. Paul. I will focus on some key texts found in John Paul II's reflections on the Sermon on the Mount in his comment on Christ's words in Matthew 5:27–28: "You have heard that it was said, 'You shall not commit adultery.' But I say to you: Whoever looks at a woman to desire [in a reductive way] her has already committed adultery with her in his heart" (cited in 46.1, pp. 309–10). These words, he declares:

> do not allow us to stop at the accusation of the human heart and to cast it into a state of continual suspicion, but that they must be understood and interpreted as an appeal addressed to the heart. *This derives from the very nature of the ethos of redemption....* Redemption is a truth ... in the name of which man must feel himself called, and "called with effectiveness." He must become aware of this call also through Christ's words ... reread in the full context of the revelation of the body. Man *must feel himself called to rediscover,* or even better, to realize, the spousal meaning of the body and to express in this way the interior freedom of the gift, that is, the freedom of that spiritual state and power that derive from mastery over the concupiscence of the flesh. (46.4, p. 312–13)

Christ's words "testify that *the original power* (and thus also the grace) *of the mystery of creation becomes* for each of them [man and woman] *the power* (that is, the grace) *of the mystery of redemption.* This concerns the very 'nature,' the very substrate of the humanity of the person, the deepest impulses of the 'heart'" (46.5, p. 313). Christ's redemptive call is to "the rediscovery of the meaning of the whole of existence, of the meaning of life, which includes also the meaning of the body that we have call 'spousal' here." Christ appeals to man's "heart", to the "supreme value, which is love", called "as a person in the truth of his humanity, and thus also in the truth of his masculinity and femininity, in the truth of his body" (46.6, p. 313–14).

"Eros", the Holy Father insists, must not be equated with lust. For Plato it "represents the inner power that draws man toward all that is good, true, and beautiful" (47.2, p. 316). It refers also to the natural and hence "good" desire experienced in the attraction of men for women and vice versa. However "erotic" desire is often identified with lust (47.3, p. 317). A proper interpretation of the Sermon on the Mount, taking into account the multiple meanings of "eros", allows us to "find room for that ethos, for those ethical and indirectly also theological contents that have been drawn in the course of our analyses from Christ's appeal to the human heart in the Sermon on the Mount" (47.4, p. 317). Christ's appeal is "the ethos of redemption. The call to what is true, good, and beautiful ['eros' in the Platonic sense] means at the same time, in the ethos of redemption, the necessity of overcoming what derives from the threefold concupiscence.... If the words of Mathew 5:27–28 represent such a call, then this means that in the erotic sphere, 'eros' and 'ethos' do not diverge, are not opposed to each other, but *are called to meet in the human heart and to bear fruit in this meeting*" (47.5, p. 318).

Ethos must become the "constituent form" of eros. "Mere desire" is quite different from a "noble pleasure," and "when sexual desire is connected with a noble pleasure, it differs from desire pure and simple" (48.4, p. 320). Only through self-control can man attain "that *deeper and more mature spontaneity* with which his 'heart,' by mastering the instincts, rediscovers the spiritual beauty of the sign constituted by the human body in its masculinity and femininity" (48.5, p. 321).

John Paul emphasizes that Christ's words in Matthew 5:27–28 must be seen in "*the perspective of the redemption* of man and the world (and thus precisely of the 'redemption of the body'). This is, in fact, the perspective of the ... whole mission of Christ"

(49.3, p. 323). In his Sermon Jesus does not invite man to return to the state of original innocence, because this has been irretrievably lost, "but *he calls him to find*—on the foundations of the perennial and . . . indestructible meanings of what is 'human'—the *living forms of the 'new man'* " (49.3, p. 323). He thus establishes continuity between the "beginning" and the perspective of redemption, for "in the ethos of the redemption of the body, the original ethos of creation was to be taken up anew" (49.4, p. 323). To achieve this redemption the man to whom Christ appeals must, with his help, be pure of heart, for "purity is a requirement of love" (49.7, p. 325).

Christ makes it clear, when he affirms (Mt 15:18–20) that what defiles a man comes from his "heart", from within himself, that "the concept of 'purity' and of 'impurity' in the moral sense is a rather general concept, not a specific one: thus, every moral good is a manifestation of purity" (50.4, p. 328). Man, male and female, is pure of heart to the degree that he has taken possession of his desires, to the degree that he has experienced the "redemption of the body" won for him by Christ and thus rediscovered its "spousal meaning" and is now able, thanks to Christ's redemptive work, to "give" himself or herself away in love and to become fully one flesh in the beautiful reality of marriage.

The Function of Spousal Meaning in the Sacrament of Love (Marriage) and in the Language of the Body

Introduction

Part Two, "The Sacrament", is divided into three chapters. In Chapter One, "The Dimension of Covenant and of Grace" (*Man and Woman* 87–102), the Holy Father considers the sacrament of marriage from the aspect of *grace and covenant*. In Chapter Two, "The Dimension of Sign" (103–17), John Paul II takes up the function of the spousal meaning of the body in the sacrament and in the "language of the body", particularly in the first two sections of this chapter—" 'Language of the Body' and the Reality of the Sign" (103–7) and "The Song of Songs" (108–13). The third section, "When the 'Language of the Body' becomes the Language of the Liturgy" (114–17), focuses on the subject indicated by its title. In the first two sections of Chapter Two the Pope shows that the "language of the body" must be reread in light of the prophetic tradition (Hosea, Ezekiel, Deutero-Isaiah and others) and of the Song of Songs, whereas in the third section he reflects on the book of Tobit. I will focus on Audiences 103–13. Thus here my focus will center on sections 1 and 2. Chapter Three of Part Two, "He Gave Them the Law of Life as Their Inheritance" (118–33) shows how the Theology of the Body is central to understanding Paul VI's teaching in *Humanae vitae* and will be considered in the final section of this chapter.

The Dimension of Sign

In the first Audience, found in Chapter Two, "'Language of the Body' and Reality of the Sign" (103), John Paul clearly identifies the subject matter of this section: "Given that the sacrament is the sign by means of which the saving reality of grace and the covenant is expressed and realized, we must now consider it under the aspect of sign, while the preceding reflections were devoted to the reality of grace and the covenant" (103.3, p. 532).

The Holy Father begins by affirming that marriage comes into being by means of the word, when the man and the woman *consent* to take each other as husband and wife. But these words "can only be fulfilled by the *copula conjugale* (conjugal intercourse). This reality (the *copula conjugale*), moreover, has been defined from the very beginning by institution of the Creator. 'A man will leave his father and his mother and unite with his wife, and the two will be one flesh' (Gen 2:24)" (103.2, p. 532). Continuing, he says:

> The words, "I take you as my wife / as my husband," bear within themselves precisely that perennial and ever unique and unrepeat-able "language of the body," and they place it at the same time in the context of the communion of persons.... In this way the

perennial and ever new "language of the body" *is not only the "substratum,"* but *in some sense also the constitutive content of persons.* The persons—the man and the woman—become a reciprocal gift for each other. They become this gift in their masculinity and femininity while they discover the spousal meaning of the body and refer it reciprocally to themselves in an irreversible way: in the dimension of life as a whole. (103.5, p. 533)

If we now "reread" the "language of the body" in light of the prophetic tradition begun by Hosea and continued by Ezekiel and others, we discover that the human body speaks a "language" whose *"author is man,* as male or female, as bridegroom or bride: man with his perennial vocation to the communion of persons". But, and this is most important, "man is *in some sense unable to express* this singular language of his personal existence and vocation *without the body.* He is constituted in such a way from the 'beginning' that the deepest words of the spirit—words of love, gift, and faithfulness—call for an appropriate 'language of the body.' And without this language, they cannot be fully expressed" (104.7, p. 537).

From this an ethical conclusion follows: In speaking the "language of the body" in truth, one must never violate its spousal meaning, its meaning as "gift". Thus the prophets testified to conjugal chastity and fidelity as the "truth" and to adultery as falsity in the "language of the body" (cf. 104.9, p. 538). The body speaks lies "through all that negates conjugal love, faithfulness, and integrity" (105.1, p. 539). John Paul says that in this way the essential truth of the sign will remain organically linked to the morality of the spouses' marital conduct (see 105.6, p. 541). Through "the whole of the 'language of the body' ... the spouses decide to speak to each other as ministers of the sacrament" (105.6, p. 541). They not only proclaim the truth coming from God, John Paul even says that they proclaim this truth *in God's name* (see 105.2, p. 539). In constituting the marital sign in the moment of consent and fulfilling it in the moment of consummation, the spouses *"perform an act of prophetic character.* They confirm in this way their share in the prophetic mission of the Church" received from Christ (105.2, p. 539).

"*There is an organic link between rereading* the integral meaning of the 'language of the body' in the truth and the consequent *use* of that language in conjugal life" (106.3, p. 543). Spouses "are explicitly called to bear witness—by correctly using the 'language of the body'—to spousal and procreative love, *a testimony worthy of 'true prophets.'* In this consists the true significance and the greatness of conjugal consent in the sacrament of the Church" (106.4, p. 544). The "greatness" of conjugal consent is precisely its prophetic witness to the "mystery hidden from eternity in God"—the mystery of Trinitarian life and love which flows through the spousal union of Christ with the Church reaching the concrete lives of men and women within history.

In the light of Christ's words in the Sermon on the Mount we know that the threefold concupiscence—of the eyes, of pride of life, and in particular the concupiscence of the flesh—"*does not destroy the capacity to reread the 'language of the body' in the truth*" (107.3, p. 546). Precisely because the body has been redeemed by Christ, "'historical' man ... is able, on the basis of the 'language of the body' reread in the truth, *to constitute the sacramental sign of* conjugal *love*, faithfulness, and integrity, and this as *an enduring sign*.... He is capable of it even as the 'man of concupiscence,' since he is at the same time 'called' by the reality of the redemption of Christ" (107.4, p. 546).

John Paul thinks that for rereading the "language of the body" in the truth "the Song of Songs has an altogether singular significance" (113.6, p. 592). The bridegroom rereads this "language" at one and the same time with his heart and with his eyes (108.8, p. 558). The bridegroom is integrated internally and externally. If a "look" determines the very intentionality of existence, the lover has determined to live in the truth of the *gift*. He respects woman as a gift. His look concentrates "on the whole female 'I' of the bride". He sees her as a *person*—a subject—created for her own sake. And her personhood "speaks to him through every feminine trait, giving rise to that state of mind that can be defined as fascination, enchantment" (108.8, p. 558).

In this way the language of the body finds a "rich echo" in the bridegroom's words. He speaks in poetic transport and metaphors, which attest to the experience of beauty, to "a love filled with pleasure" (108.8, p. 559). The bridegroom says, "You are all beautiful, my friend, and there is no spot in you" (Song 4:7). And further on he calls her "my perfect one" (Song 5:2). John Paul tells us that the bridegroom's desire, "born from love on the basis of the 'language of the body' is a search for integral beauty, for purity free from every stain; it is a search for perfection that contains ... *the synthesis of human beauty, beauty of soul and body*" (112.3. p. 584).

John Paul continues: "And if the words of the bridegroom just quoted ['Open to me ... my perfect one'] seem to contain the distant echo of the 'beginning'—that first search-aspiration of the male man for a being still unknown—they resound much nearer in Ephesians where Christ, as Bridegroom of the Church, desires to see his Bride without 'spot,' desires to see her 'holy and immaculate' (Eph 5:27)" (112.3, p. 584).

As Christopher West says in his superb commentary,

> In other words, the bridegroom of the Song, like Christ, points us in two directions. He points us back to the beginning, to God's original plan for married love, and to the eschatological future when the Marriage of the Lamb will be consummated. Then the Bride will be made *perfect forever*. She will shine radiantly—without blemish, wrinkle, or any such thing (see Eph 5:27). Then, in the Marriage of the Lamb, we will discover the true, integral beauty of everyone who forms the great communion of saints. It will be a beauty "free from every stain," a "*beauty of soul and body*," as John Paul says. And this dazzling beauty of every human being will be but a dim reflection, a little glimmer of the beauty of the Eternal One whom we will behold "face to face."[7]

The bridegroom frequently refers to the bride first of all as his "sister": "You have ravished my heart, my sister, my bride; you have ravished my heart with one glance of your eyes.... How sweet are your caresses, my sister, my bride" (Song 4:9–10). Commenting on this language the Holy Father says that this way of

[7] West, *Theology of the Body Explained*, p. 483.

speaking says much more than if he had called her by her proper name. They show how love reveals the other person. "The fact that in this approach the feminine 'I' is revealed for the bridegroom as 'sister'—and that *she is bride* precisely *as sister*—has a particular eloquence" (109.4, p. 562). These words show that the bridegroom does not see her as a thing to be appropriated, but as a *person* to be loved. To be a person "means both 'being a subject,' but also 'being in relation'" (109.4, p. 562). The term "sister" denotes this. It speaks of the two different ways in which masculinity and femininity "incarnate" the same humanity, and it speaks of their being in reciprocal relationship. The bridegroom can also be regarded as "brother", indeed the bride declares: "O that you were a brother to me, who nursed at my mother's breast!" (Song 8:1). Recognizing each other as brother and sister challenges the man to see whether he is motivated by love, by the sincere gift of self, or by lust, a desire to gratify himself. The bridegroom accepts this challenge and gives a spontaneous answer to it (109.4, p. 562): "Do not stir up, do not awaken the beloved until she wants it!" (Song 8:4).

John Paul says that the "bridegroom's words tend to reproduce ... the history of the femininity of the beloved person; they see her still in the time of girlhood ('We have a little sister, and she still has no breasts')". In this way, his words "embrace her entire 'I,' soul and body, *with a disinterested tenderness*" (110.2, p. 566). This same tenderness carries through when the term "sister" gives way to the term "bride". The transition from "sister" to "bride" maintains—and it must maintain—the same recognition of her personhood, of her dignity as "sister". In fact, "through marriage man and woman become brother and sister in a special way" (114.3 p. 594).

From the Holy Father's analysis of the "language of the body" reread in the truth, it follows that spouses redeemed in Christ will never "look" at one another "to desire them", thereby committing "adultery in the heart". From this we can also see how this part of *Man and Woman* deepens our understanding of the truths present in the Audiences devoted to God's original plan and to Christ's appeal to the human heart.

The "Language of the Body" and the Defense of Humanae Vitae

Audiences 118–33 are devoted to John Paul II's defense of *Humanae vitae*. Audiences 118–25 take up *The Ethical Problem* and I will limit my presentation to these.

John Paul II begins by focusing attention on Paul VI's affirmation that there is an inseparable connection between the unitive and procreative meanings of the conjugal act (*Humanae vitae*, no. 12). He points out that these words "concern the moment in the common life of the couple in which the two, by being united in the conjugal act, become 'one flesh'" (118.4, p. 619). After summarizing relevant teaching from *Humanae vitae* and the Second Vatican Council's Pastoral Constitution on the Church in the Modern World (119–22) John Paul shows how the "language of the body" is related to this Church teaching. "The human body", he declares, is "the means of the expression of man as an integral whole, of the person, which reveals itself through 'the language of the body'" (123.2, p. 631). Then focusing attention on the "personalistic" dimension of the problem (which he distinguishes from the sacramental or theological while nevertheless in no way separating them), he notes that man is subject of the natural law in the integral truth of his subjectivity and that revelation shows that he has been called by God to be a witness and interpreter of the eternal plan of love by becoming the minister of the sacrament that from the "beginning" has been constituted in the sign of the "union of the flesh" (123.3, p. 632).

In a key passage he then emphasizes that as ministers of the sacrament constituted by consent and perfected by conjugal union "man and woman are called *to express* the mysterious *'language' of their bodies in all the truth that properly belongs to it.*" Moreover, according to the truth of the "language of the body" the conjugal act means not only love but also potential fruitfulness. From this it follows that the act is deprived of its proper fullness, of the truth, if its potential fruitfulness is intentionally violated. "Such a violation of the inner order of conjugal communion, a communion that plunges its roots into the very order of the person, *constitutes the essential evil of the contraceptive act"* (123.4 and 7, pp. 632 and 633).

The reasoning given here to show the evil of contraception, as can be seen, is somewhat different from although surely in harmony with the reasoning we discovered in *Love and Responsibility*, namely, that in order for the conjugal act to conform to the personalistic norm those engaging in it must be willing to become fathers and mothers and obviously they are not so willing if they contracept. But it is also obvious, it seems to me, that when spouses intentionally repudiate the fruitfulness of the conjugal act and thereby violate the "inner order of conjugal communion", as John Paul II argues in *Man and Woman*, they surely are not willing to become parents in this act. The reasoning also differs somewhat but is closely linked to the reasoning we saw used in *Familiaris Consortio* 32, where John Paul emphasized that contraception is evil because it is a lie insofar as in it the spouses refuse to "give" themselves to one another in the conjugal act, thereby falsifying the "language of the body". But again it seems obvious that by violating the "inner order of conjugal communion" they are failing to give themselves unreservedly to one another.

7

Pope Benedict XVI's Teaching on Marriage and Family Life

Joseph Cardinal Ratzinger was elected on April 19, 2005, to succeed John Paul II as the Bishop of Rome, Christ's Vicar on earth, the Pope, our Holy Father. On election he chose Benedict XVI as his name. In 2007 *L'Osservatore Romano* published a booklet entitled *La Verità sulla famiglia: Matrimonio e unioni di fatto nelle parole di Benedetto XVI*, which included eighteen Addresses of Pope Benedict on marriage and the family given between May 17, 2005, and February 4, 2007. Of the eighteen addresses printed in *L'Osservatore Romano*'s booklet, five seemed to me to be of greater significance; thus I will offer summaries of them here, using the English translations found on the Vatican website.[1] I will then summarize his teaching on marriage in his first encyclical, *Deus caritas est, God Is Love.*

1. Benedict's Papal Addresses Relevant for His Teaching on Marriage and Family

The following addresses are the most significant: 1. Address to Participants in the Ecclesial Diocesan Convention of Rome, June

---

[1] Of course, during 2008, the fortieth anniversary of Pope Paul VI's Encyclical *Human vitae*, Pope Benedict gave many other additional addresses and homilies strongly affirming the Church's teaching on marriage and the need for every marital act to be open to the gift of human life.

6, 2005; 2. Address to Members of the Pontifical John Paul II
Institute for Studies on Marriage and Family on the 25th Anniversary of Its Founding, May 11, 2006; 3. Address to Participants
in the Plenary Session of the Pontifical Council for the Family,
May 13, 2006; 4. Address to the Fifth World Meeting of Families, Valencia, Spain, July 8, 2006; and 5. Address to Members of
the Tribunal of the Roman Rota, January 27, 2007. Before looking at them individually, I think it is a good idea to identify elements common to almost all of them.

The most important common element is that Pope Benedict
for the most part simply reaffirms strongly the constant teaching
of the Magisterium on marriage and the family, invoking in particular the teaching of his predecessor Pope John Paul II, including the teaching John Paul set forth in his audiences on the
Theology of the Body. Another element common to many of his
addresses is Benedict XVI's identification of errors concerning
marriage and the family that he sees rooted in a relativistic misunderstanding of marriage and family life and indeed of the human
person.

*1. Address to Participants in the Ecclesial Diocesan Convention of
Rome* (June 6, 2005)

This is the longest of the addresses found in *L'Osservatore Romano's*
booklet, approximately 3,500 words. It was given at the Roman
diocesan convention devoted to the theme, "Family and Christian community formation of the person and transmission of the
faith". This was the focus of Benedict's address, in which he referred
in particular to Part II, nos. 12–16 of John Paul's apostolic exhortation *Familiaris consortio*, the part devoted to "The Plan of God
for Marriage and the Family".

At the beginning of his reflections Benedict emphasized that
the question concerning the right relationship between man and
woman "is rooted in the essential core of the human being and it
is only by starting from here that its response can be found". This

requires us to ask: Who is man? And who is God? The Bible answers by instructing us as follows: "Man is made in the image of God and that God himself is love. It is therefore the vocation to love that makes the human person an authentic image of God: man and woman come to resemble God to the extent that they become loving people."

"This fundamental connection", he continued, in an important passage emphasizing the *bodily* nature of the human person,

> between God and the person gives rise to another: the indissolu- ble connection between spirit and body: in fact, the human being is a soul that finds expression in a body and a body that is enliv- ened by an immortal spirit. The body, therefore, both male and female, also has, as it were, a theological character: it is not merely a body; and what is biological in the human being is not merely biological but is the expression and the fulfilment of our human- ity. Likewise, human sexuality is not juxtaposed to our being as person but part of it. Only when sexuality is integrated within the person does it successfully acquire meaning. Thus, these two links, between the human being with God and, in the human being, of the body with the spirit, give rise to a third: the con- nection between the person and the institution [of marriage].

Benedict then goes on to stress that human freedom of choice enables a man and a woman to give to one another an uncon- ditional "gift" of themselves as sexual, bodily persons in getting married. Then, in a passage reaffirming John Paul II's teaching in *Familiaris consortio* 12, he declares:

> the personal and reciprocal "yes" of the man and the woman makes room for the future, for the authentic humanity of each of them. At the same time, it is an assent to the gift of a new life. Therefore, this personal "yes" must also be a publicly respon- sible "yes", with which the spouses take on the public respon- sibility of fidelity, also guaranteeing the future of the community. None of us, in fact, belongs exclusively to himself or herself; one and all are therefore called to take on in their inmost depths their own public responsibility. Marriage as an institution is thus not an undue interference of society or of authority. The exter- nal imposition of form on the most private reality of life is instead

an intrinsic requirement of the covenant of conjugal love and of
the depths of the human person [cf. *Familiaris consortio*, 12].

After identifying various ways in which marriage is eroded
today—free unions, "trial marriages", attempts of same sex persons to marry—all based on a pseudo-freedom, he affirms that
the truth about marriage and the family, rooted in the truth about
the human person "has been actuated in salvation history" to
such an extent that "God could take the history of love and of
the union of a man and a woman in the covenant of marriage as
a symbol of salvation history. The inexpressible fact, the mystery
of God's love for men and women, receives its linguistic form
from the vocabulary of marriage and the family." He then focuses
on the sacramentality of Christian marriage, declaring:

> In the New Testament God radicalizes his love to the point that he
> himself becomes, in his Son, flesh of our flesh, a true man. In this
> way, God's union with humankind acquired its supreme, irrevers-
> ible form. Thus, the blueprint of human love is also definitely set
> out, that reciprocal "yes" which cannot be revoked; it does not
> alienate men and women but sets them free from the different forms
> of alienation in history in order to restore them to the truth of
> creation. The sacramental quality that marriage assumes in Christ,
> therefore, means that the gift of creation has been raised to the
> grace of redemption. Christ's grace is not an external addition to
> human nature, it does not do violence to men and women but sets
> them free and restores them, precisely by raising them above their
> own limitations. And just as the Incarnation of the Son of God
> reveals its true meaning in the Cross, so genuine human love is
> self-giving and cannot exist if it seeks to detach itself from the Cross.

The contemporary debasement of marriage and human love and
the desire to "liberate" human nature from God, the Pope says,
leads to a debasement of the human person. He then strongly
reaffirms Church teaching on the bond between marriage and
the gift of new human life and the immorality of contraception.

> Even in the begetting of children marriage reflects its divine model,
> God's love for man. In man and woman, fatherhood and moth-
> erhood, like the body and like love, cannot be limited to the

biological; life is entirely given only when, by birth, love and meaning are also given, which make it possible to say yes to this life. From this point it becomes clear how contrary to human love, to the profound vocation of the man and the woman, are the systematic closure of a union to the gift of life and even more, the suppression or manipulation of newborn life.

The larger family of the Church supports and nurtures the family, Benedict adds and the Church "is reciprocally built up by the family, a 'small domestic church,' as the Second Vatican Council called it (*Lumen gentium*, no. 11; *Apostolicam actuositatem*, no. 11)". Benedict then notes that John Paul's *Familiaris consortio* (15) affirms in the same way that Christian marriage "constitutes the natural setting in which the human person is introduced into the great family of the Church".

In carrying out their mission to educate their children parents must keep in mind that prayer, which is "personal friendship with Christ and contemplation in him of the face of the Father, is indispensably at the root of the formation of the Christian and of the transmission of the faith", and in this work they need the help of the larger Church, of the parish, diocese, priests and religious. This task is made more difficult today because of the cultural relativism that dominates much of our world, Benedict says. Thus toward the conclusion of his address he issued a challenge:

> [N]ot only must we seek to get the better of relativism in our work of forming people, but we are also called to counter its destructive predominance in society and culture. Hence, as well as the words of the Church, the witness and public commitment of Christian families is very important, especially in order to reassert the inviolability of human life from conception until its natural end, the unique and irreplaceable value of the family founded on marriage and the need for legislative and administrative measures that support families in the task of bringing children into the world and raising them, an essential duty for our common future.

In concluding he asked for prayers for vocations to the priesthood and religious life, taking care to note the key role that Christian families play in nurturing such vocations.

2. Address to Members of the Pontifical John Paul II Institute for Studies on Marriage and Family on the 25th Anniversary of Its Founding (May 11, 2006)

Although brief, only a little over two thousand words, this address is rich in content, and was given to celebrate the twenty-fifth anniversary of John Paul II's founding of his Pontifical Institute for Studies on Marriage and Family (which now has branches in Rome; Washington, D.C.; Valencia, Spain; as well as in several cities in Mexico; Benin, Brazil; Kerala, India; and Melbourne, Australia). In it Benedict offers a splendid summary of John Paul II's legacy regarding marriage and the family. It is so excellent it needs to be cited in full:

> As a young priest, Karol Wojtyla already had the idea of "teaching how to love". It was later to fill him with enthusiasm when, as a young Bishop, he confronted the difficult times that followed the publication of my predecessor Paul VI's prophetic and ever timely Encyclical *Humanae Vitae*.
>
> It was then that he realized the need for a systematic study of this topic. It was the basis of this teaching which he later offered to the entire Church in his unforgettable *Catechesis on human love* [given in TOB audiences September 1979–November 1984]. Thus, *two* fundamental *elements* were highlighted that in recent years you have sought to examine more deeply and that give novelty to your Institute as an academic reality with a specific mission in the Church.
>
> The *first element* concerns the fact that marriage and the family are rooted in the inmost nucleus of the truth about man and his destiny. Sacred Scripture reveals that the vocation to love is part of the authentic image of God which the Creator has desired to impress upon his creatures, calling them to resemble him precisely to the extent in which they are open to love.
>
> Consequently, the sexual difference that distinguishes the male from the female body is not a mere biological factor but has a far deeper significance. It expresses that form of love with which man and woman, by becoming one flesh, as Sacred Scripture says, can achieve

an authentic communion of people open to the transmission of life and who thus cooperate with God in the procreation of new human beings.

A *second element* marks the newness of John Paul II's teaching on human love: his original way of interpreting God's plan precisely in the convergence of divine revelation with the human experience. Indeed, in Christ, fullness of the revelation of the Father's love, is also expressed the full truth of the human vocation to love that can only be found completely in the sincere gift of self.

Benedict then drew attention to what he had to say about marriage in his first encyclical, *Deus caritas est*. There he emphasized that it is precisely through love that "the Christian image of God and the resulting image of mankind and its destiny" (no. 1) shines forth. In other words, God used the way of love to reveal the intimate mystery of his Trinitarian life. Furthermore, the close relationship that exists between the image of God-Love and human love enables us to understand that "[c]orresponding to the image of a monotheistic God is monogamous marriage. Marriage based on exclusive and definitive love becomes the icon of the relationship between God and his people and vice versa. God's way of loving becomes the measure of human love" (no. 11). We will consider his teaching in that encyclical later.

3. Address to Participants in the Plenary Session of the Pontifical Council for the Family (May 13, 2006)

In this brief address (a little over a thousand words) Benedict stressed the "well-know principles of marriage". The first is that the family founded on marriage "is the vital cell and pillar of society ... a reality that all States must hold in the highest regard because, as John Paul II liked to repeat, 'the future of humanity passes by way of the family'" (*Familiaris consortio*, no. 86). The second principle is that Christians know that Christ has raised marriage to the dignity of a sacrament. Thus he "confers greater splendour and depth on the conjugal bond and more powerfully binds the spouses who, blessed by the Lord of the Covenant, promise each other faithfulness until death in love that is open to life".

The third is that Christ accompanies spouses in their life with the result that the Christian family "not only cooperates with God in generating natural life, but also in cultivating the seeds of divine life given in Baptism".

After noting the widespread influence of erroneous views that debase the human person, authentic freedom, and marriage, Benedict called particular attention to the respect due to the human embryo, which ought always to be born from an act of love and should always be treated as a person (cf. Pope John Paul II's encyclical *Evangelium vitae*, no. 60). He then reminded his audience that *Humanae vitae* clearly taught that "human procreation must always be the fruit of the conjugal act with its twofold unitive and procreative meaning (cf. no. 12)." The greatness of conjugal love in accordance with the divine plan demands this, he said. He had, he noted, recalled this truth in his encyclical *Deus caritas est* when he wrote: "*Eros* reduced to pure 'sex', has become a commodity, a mere 'thing' to be bought and sold, or rather, man himself becomes a commodity. . . . Here we are actually dealing with a debasement of the human body (no. 5)".

4. *Address to the Fifth World Meeting of Families* (Valencia, Spain, July 8, 2006)

This address is also relatively short (about two thousand words) but rich in content and covering a good deal of material relevant to marriage and family. The pope said that the Church constantly seeks to show her pastoral concern for the family which is so basic to the human person. In the *Compendium of the Catechism of the Catholic Church*, 337, the Magisterium teaches that "God, who is love and who created man and woman for love, has called them to love ... to an intimate communion of life and love in Marriage. 'So they are no longer two but one flesh'

(Mt 19:6)." And he reminded the participants that John Paul II had said that "man has been made 'in the image and likeness of God not only by his being human, but also by the communion of the persons that man and woman have formed since the beginning. They become the image of God, not so much in their aloneness as in their communion'" (a citation Benedict made from John Paul's Catechesis on the TOB given on November 14, 1979).

Benedict said nothing can take the place of the family, which is based primarily on a deep interpersonal relationship between husband and wife that is enabled by the help given to them by God in the sacrament of matrimony, "a true vocation to holiness". The family is an indispensable foundation for society, a great and lifelong treasure for couples, and a unique good for children, who are meant to be the fruit of the love, of the total and generous self-giving of their parents. "To proclaim the whole truth about the family, based on marriage as *a domestic Church and a sanctuary of life*, is a great responsibility incumbent upon all."

He stressed that "[f]ather and mother have said a complete 'yes' in the sight of God, which constitutes the basis of the sacrament which joins them together.... [T]hey also need to say a 'yes' of acceptance to the children whom they have given birth to or adopted, and each of which has his or her own personality and character."

He continued by noting that the challenges of modern society make it necessary to ensure that families do not feel alone. "The ecclesial community therefore has the responsibility of offering support, encouragement, and spiritual nourishment which can strengthen the cohesiveness of the family, especially in times of trial or difficulty." Christ has shown us that the supreme source of our life and the lives of families is love: "This is my commandment, that you love one another as I have loved you" (Jn 15:12). This love has been poured into us at baptism and "families are called to experience this same kind of love, for the Lord makes it possible for us, through our human love, to be sensitive, loving and merciful...."

5. Address to Members of the Tribunal of the Roman Rota (January 27, 2007)

In this address Pope Benedict noted that some people think that "the conciliar teaching on marriage, and in particular, the description of this institution as '*intima communitas vitae et amoris*' [the intimate partnership of life and love (*Gaudium et spes*, no. 48)], must lead to a denial of the existence of an indissoluble conjugal bond because this would be a question of an 'ideal' to which 'normal Christians' cannot be 'constrained'." The Council did indeed describe marriage in this way, but, as the Pope went on to emphasize, this intimate partnership of life and love "is determined, in accordance with the tradition of the Church, by a whole set of principles of the divine law which establish its true and permanent anthropological meaning".

The development of this Conciliar teaching by Popes Paul VI and John Paul II "was based on the indisputable presupposition that marriage has a truth of its own—that is, the human knowledge, illumined by the Word of God, of the sexually different reality of the man and of the woman with their profound needs for complementarity, definitive self-giving and exclusivity—to whose discovery and deepening reason and faith harmoniously contribute". Continuing, Benedict stresses that the *anthropological and saving truth of marriage*, including its juridical dimension, is rooted in the New Testament, in Jesus' appeal to the "beginning" in his reply to the Pharisees who put him to the test by asking him about the lawfulness of divorces (cf. Mt 19:4–6). He then noted that "The citations of Genesis (1:27; 2:24) propose the matrimonial truth of the 'principle', that truth whose fullness is found in connection with Christ's union with the Church (cf. Eph 5:30–31) and was the object of such broad and deep reflections on the part of Pope John Paul II in his cycles of catecheses on human love in the divine design."

"Every marriage", the pope declares, "is of course the result of the free consent of the man and the woman, but in practice their freedom expresses the natural capacity inherent in their masculinity and femininity.

"The union takes place by virtue of the very plan of God who created them male and female and gives them the power to unite for ever those natural and complementary dimensions of their persons. The indissolubility of marriage does not derive from the definitive commitment of those who contract it but is intrinsic in the nature of the 'powerful bond established by the Creator'" (John Paul II, Catechesis on the TOB, General Audience November 21, 1979, no. 2).

The juridical dimension of marriage is quite striking, Benedict points out, in St. Paul's teaching on marriage. In his profound treatment of the "mysterion mega" in Ephesians 5, in which he compares the love between husband and wife to Christ's love for his bride the Church, St. Paul "did not hesitate to apply to marriage the strongest legal terms to designate the juridical bond by which spouses are united in their sexual dimension." In this Pauline perspective and in the Church's tradition, Benedict then affirms that

> law is truly interwoven with life and love as one of the intrinsic obligations of its existence. Therefore, as I wrote in my first Encyclical, "From the standpoint of creation, *eros* directs man towards marriage, to a bond which is unique and definitive; thus, and only thus, does it fulfil its deepest purpose" (*Deus caritas est*, no. 11).

> Thus, love and law can be united to the point of ensuring that husband and wife *mutually owe to one another* the love *with which they spontaneously love one another:* the love in them is the fruit of their free desire for the good of one another and of their children; which, moreover, is also a requirement of love for one's own true good.

> All the activity of the Church and of the faithful in the context of the family must be based on this *truth about marriage and its intrinsic juridical dimension.*

He concludes his address to the members of the tribunal of the Roman Rota by noting the devastating effects today of a culture of relativism that would make marriage something dependent on the subjective feelings of people at different times and not on God's loving plan. "One must react to this tendency", he says, "with courage and faith, constantly applying the *hermeneutic of renewal in continuity* and not allowing oneself to be seduced by forms of interpretation that involve a break with the Church's tradition."

2. The Encyclical *Deus Caritas Est* on the Love (*Amor*) between Man and Woman as Uniting *Eros* and *Agape*

In his first encyclical, *Deus caritas est*, Pope Benedict XVI wished "to speak of the love [*amor*] which God lavishes upon us and which we in turn must share with others" (no. 1).[2] Noting the "vast semantic range of the word 'love' (*amor*)", he then said:

> Amid this multiplicity of meanings, ... one in particular stands out: love [*amor*] between man and woman, where body and soul are inseparably joined and human beings glimpse an apparently irresistible promise of happiness. This would seem to be the very epitome of love [*amoris per excellentiam imago perfecta*]; all other kinds of love [*cetera universa amoris genera*] seem to fade in comparison. So we need to ask: are all these forms of love [*omnesne amoris hae formae*] basically one, so that love [*amor*], in its many and varied manifestations, is ultimately a single reality, or are we merely using the same word to designate totally different realities?
> (*Deus caritas est*, no. 2)

I have inserted the Latin word *amor* in parentheses in this passage because the Latin text of the Encyclical uses several different words for "love": the title uses *caritas*, the word used in the Latin text of Scripture to translate the Greek *agape*. In citing Scripture the Latin

[2] Much of the following text on Pope Benedict XVI's teaching on marriage is taken by the author from his essay on his Encyclical *Deus caritas est*, which was published in Italian as "L'amore fra uomo e donna: archetipo di amore par excellenza" in *La Via dell'Amore: Riflessioni sull'enciclica "Deus caritas est" di Benedetto XVI*, edited by Livio Melina and Carl Anderson (Rome: Pontificio Istituto Giovanni Paolo II per Studi su Matimonio e Famiglia, 2006), pp. 47–58. The English translation was published as "Love between Man and Woman as the Epitome of Love" in *The Way of Love* (San Francisco: Ignatius Press, 2006), pp. 66–69. This edition was © 2006 by the John Paul II Institute for Studies on Marriage and the Family, and is reprinted by permission of Monsignor Livio Melina.

text of the Encyclical uses the verb *diligo* to translate the Greek *agapao*, e.g., *"Sic enim* dilexit *Deus mundum, ut Filium suum unigenitum daret Deus caritas est, ..."* (Jn 3:16; no. 1) ("God so *loved* the world that he gave his only Son ..."). But, and it is most important to note this, the Latin text of the Encyclical more frequently uses the Latin noun *amor* and the Latin verb *amo* to speak of God's love for man: e.g. *"in his Nostris primis Encyclicis Litteris de* amore *cupimus loqui quo Deus nos replet quique a nobis cum aliis communicari debet"* (no. 1); *"Dei* amor *nobis quaestio est de vita principalis"* (no. 2); *"Deus hic hominem* amat*"* (no. 9). In fact, Pope Benedict says, "Since God has first loved [*dilexit*] us (cf. 1 Jn 4:10), love (*amor*) is now no longer a mere 'command'; it is the response to the gift of love with which God draws near to us [*verum est responsio erga* amoris *donum, quo Deus nobis occurrit*]" (no. 1).

In Latin, consequently, the word *amor* is the more universal word for "love", and is so used in the official Latin text of Benedict's Encyclical. In fact, in the first part of the document Pope Benedict argues that *amor* integrates into one the different kinds of "love" identified by the Greek words *eros* and *agape*. Here I will not attempt to summarize his entire argument but will rather focus on those elements of it concerned with showing how authentic love *(amor)* between man and woman unites *eros* and *agape*.

After noting that "the love [*amor*] between man and woman which is neither planned nor willed, but somehow imposes itself upon human beings, was called *eros* by the ancient Greeks" (*Deus caritas est*, no. 3), the Pope is subsequently at pains to show that biblical faith in no way rejects *eros* as such. While declaring "war on a warped and destructive form" of *eros* (no. 4), biblical faith leads us to understand that there is an underlying unity between *eros* or "ascending" love and *agape* or "descending" love.

Thus in his reflections on the *Song of Songs*, whose poems were "originally love-songs [*cantus amoris*], perhaps intended for a Jewish wedding feast and meant to exalt conjugal love [*coniugalis amor*]", Benedict says,

> Love [*amor*] now becomes concern and care for the other. No longer is it self-seeking, a sinking in the intoxication of happiness;

instead it seeks the good of the beloved: it becomes renunciation and it is ready, and even willing, for sacrifice.

It is part of love's [*amoris*] growth towards higher levels and inward purification that it now seeks to become definitive, and it does so in a twofold sense: both in the sense of exclusivity (this particular person alone) and in the sense of being "for ever".... Love is indeed "ecstasy", not in the sense of a moment of intoxication, but rather as a journey, an ongoing exodus out of the closed inward-looking self towards its liberation through self-giving, and thus towards authentic self-discovery and indeed the discovery of God. "Whoever seeks to gain his life will lose it, but whoever loses his life will preserve it" (Lk 17:33), as Jesus says throughout the Gospels (cf. Mt 10:39; 16:25; Mk 8:35; Lk 9:24; Jn 12:25). In these words, Jesus portrays his own path, which leads through the Cross to the Resurrection: the path of the grain of wheat that falls to the ground and dies, and in this way bears much fruit. Starting from the depths of his own sacrifice and of the love [*amoris*] that reaches fulfill-ment therein, he also portrays in these words the essence of love [*amoris essentiam*] and indeed of human life itself. (*Deus caritas est*, no. 6)

He emphasizes that "the more the two [*eros* and *agape*], in their different aspects, find a proper unity in the one reality [*veritate*] of love [*amoris*], the more the true nature of love [*vera amoris natura*] in general is realized. Even if *eros* is at first mainly covetous and ascending ... in drawing near to the other, it is less and less con-cerned with itself, increasingly seeks the happiness of the other, is concerned more and more with the beloved, bestows itself and wants to 'be there for' the other". (No. 7)

In commenting on the Genesis accounts of creation the Pope declares: "[F]rom the standpoint of creation, *eros* directs man towards marriage, to a bond which is unique and definitive; thus, and only thus, does it fulfill its deepest purpose. Corresponding to the image of a monotheistic God is monogamous marriage. Mar-riage based on exclusive and definitive love (*in amore unico et definito fundatur*) becomes the icon of the relationship between God and his people and vice versa. God's way of loving (*ratio qua Deus amat* [e.g., as the passionate lover and spouse of Israel (Hosea,

Ezekiel; cf. *Deus caritas est*, no. 9) whose love is at once both *eros* and *agape*] becomes the measure of human love (*humani amoris*)" (no. 11).

From all this we can see that when Pope Benedict declares that the "love (*amor*) between man and woman" is the "very epitome of love", the love he is talking about is the love between husband and wife, i.e., marital or conjugal love, *amor coniugalis*. This love, moreover, has an essentially *bodily* component: Thus in the text already cited in which he proclaims the "love (*amor*) between man and woman" to be "the very epitome of love", Benedict had emphasized that in this love "body and soul are inseparably joined" (*Deus caritas est*, no. 2). And later in the encyclical he stressed that "man is a being made up of body and soul ... [and] is truly himself when his body and soul are intimately united; the challenge of *eros* can be said to be truly overcome when this unification is achieved ... [and that] Christian faith ... has always considered man a unity in duality, a reality in which spirit and matter compenetrate, and in which each is brought to a new nobility" (no. 5).

In 2008 Pope Benedict XVI deepened his teaching on marriage in many addresses commemorating the 40th anniversary of Paul VI's reaffirmation of Church teaching in his great encyclical *Humanae vitae* on marriage and the sublime privilege of spouses to cooperate with God in giving life, love, and education to new human persons. In his 2009 encyclical *Caritas in veritate* he also devoted several important passages to reaffirm this teaching, in particular in view of "new reproductive technologies" that divorce the generation of human life from the conjugal embrace of loving spouses.

Conclusion

Pope Benedict XVI's teaching on marriage, as can be seen from the material presented here, is in perfect continuity with the Catholic magisterial tradition, and it draws much not only from the teaching of the Second Vatican Council but also and especially from the teaching of Pope John Paul II—in particular, it should be noted, from the late pontiff's mind-expanding and biblically rooted catecheses on the Theology of the Body. Like John Paul, Benedict is very clear in emphasizing that human persons are *bodily beings*, whose bodies are integral to their *being* as persons. In identifying the major root of the contemporary culture of death John Paul II focused on the dualism pervading that culture, a dualism that divides the "person" from his or her body, regarding the latter as a privileged instrument *of* the person, a useful good *extrinsic* to the person but in no way a *good intrinsic* to the *being* of the human person. Benedict is in full agreement with this but he moreover focuses attention on the cultural and moral relativism that dominates modern societies, in particular the Western democracies. He thus challenges us to resist this dualism with all the sources available; this is a necessary step in the re-evangelization so sorely needed today.

Pope John Paul II's *Letter to Families*: An Overview

Pope John Paul II's *Letter to Families*, dated February 2, 1994, was written to express the Church's concern for families during the International Year of the Family. The *Letter to Families*, hereafter referred to as *Letter*, contains an Introduction (numbered sections 1–5) and two major parts: I. "The Civilization of Love" (numbered sections 6–17), and II. "The Bridegroom Is with You" (numbered sections 18–23). In the *Letter* the Holy Father, who throughout his entire life as a priest and in a special way throughout his pontificate devoted extraordinary attention to marriage and family, speaks passionately about the absolutely indispensable role that the family, rooted in the marriage of one man and one woman, has to play in the "civilization of love". His burning desire is to awaken in the hearts and minds of men and women, and in particular in the hearts and minds of Christian spouses, an understanding of and commitment to the sublime mission entrusted by God to families, to encourage husbands and wives to be faithful to their vocation, and to defend the family from the dangers threatening it today.

This *Letter*, written after John Paul II had finished his catecheses on the Theology of the Body, is noteworthy in that in it John Paul II recapitulates and/or deepens major ideas and themes set forth in those catecheses (see Chapter Six, above). Here, however, I will not focus on this aspect of this wonderful letter. Rather, I will try to provide an overview of the *Letter* by focusing on the following themes developed in it: (1) the meaning of the "civilization of love"; (2) marriage as the "rock" upon which the family is built precisely because it is a person-affirming, love-enabling, life-giving, and sanctifying reality, and (3) the family and society.

The Meaning of the "Civilization of Love"

"The civilization of love", the Holy Father writes, "originates in the revelation of the God who 'is love', as John writes (cf. 1 Jn 4:8, 16) ... and it grows as a result of the *constant cultivation* which the Gospel allegory of the vine and the branches describes in such a direct way: 'I am the true vine, and my Father is the vinedresser. Every branch of mine that bears no fruit, he takes away, and every branch that bears fruit he prunes, that it may bear more fruit' (Jn 15:1–2)" (*Letter*, no. 13).

God, who "is love", created man out of love and for love. "No living being on earth except man [male and female] was created 'in the image and likeness of God'" (Gen 1:26–27) (no. 6), from whose hands he "has received the world ... together with the task of shaping it in his own image and likeness. The fulfillment of this task gives rise to civilization, which in the final analysis is nothing else than the 'humanization of the world'" (no. 13).

Moreover, and most importantly, the Holy Father, citing from *Gaudium et spes*, reminds us that "by his incarnation the Son of God united himself in a certain way to every man" and in fact "fully discloses man to himself" (no. 22). From this it follows that the civilization of love culminates in the redemptive, self-giving love of God that has been fully revealed to us in the life, death, and Resurrection of his only-begotten Son. As a being made by the God who is love and as a being whose vocation is to love even as we have been and are loved by God in Christ, man can find himself, fulfill himself, only through love, which essentially consists in the "sincere gift of self" (*Letter*, no. 11; cf. *Gaudium et spes*, no. 24).

And *"the family is fundamental to ... the 'civilization of love'"* (*Letter*, no. 13). The family, in fact, *"is the center and the heart of the civilization of love"*, a civilization completely dependent on the truth about man and his vocation (no. 13). But what is the family, and why is it the center and heart of the civilization of love?

Marriage: The "Rock" on Which the Family Is Built

The Holy Father says that his *Letter* is "in the first place ... a prayer to Christ to remain in every human family" (no. 4), and that "prayer should first of all be an encouraging witness on the part of those families who live out their human and Christian vocation in the communion of the home." "With reason it can be said that these families make up 'the norm', even admitting the existence of more than a few 'irregular situations'." Continuing, he says, "And experience shows what an important role is played by a family living in accordance with the moral norm, so that the individual born and raised in it will be able to set out without hesitation on the road of the good, which *is always written in the heart*" (no. 5).

The family "living in accordance with the moral norm" is the family built upon the marriage of one man and one woman. Indeed,

> marriage, which undergirds the institution of the family, is constituted by the covenant whereby "a man and a woman establish between themselves a partnership of their whole life," and which "of its own very nature is ordered to the well-being of the spouses and to the procreation and upbringing of children" (*Code of Canon Law*, Canon 1055, par. 1; *Catechism of the Catholic Church*, no. 1601). Only such a union can be recognized and ratified as a "marriage" in society. Other interpersonal unions which do not fulfil the above conditions cannot be recognized, despite certain growing trends which represent a serious threat to the future of the family and of society itself (no. 17).

This is the family whose *"primordial model"*, as we can see "[i]n the light of the New Testament ... *is to be sought in God himself, in the Trinitarian mystery of his life.* The divine 'We' is the eternal pattern of the human 'we', especially of that 'we' formed by the man and the woman created in the divine image and likeness" (no. 6). For marriage is God's great gift to mankind, created by him and given its defining characteristics by him in the act of creating man—male and female. This is precisely the meaning of the first chapters of Genesis, which John Paul II elsewhere speaks of as the narratives relating the "beatifying beginning" of the human race.[1] The marriage of one man and one woman is the "rock" on which the family in its normative sense is built because marriage is a *person-affirming*, *love-enabling*, and *life-giving reality*. Moreover, because this beautiful human reality has been raised by Christ to the dignity of a sacrament of the new law of love, it is also a *sanctifying reality*.

1. Marriage: A Person-affirming Reality

Marriage is a person-affirming reality because it "is a covenant of persons in love" (*Letter*, no. 7). It comes into existence when a man and a woman, forswearing all others, *give themselves to each other irrevocably as husband and wife*. It is rooted in a free, self-determining choice whereby the man, in giving himself unconditionally to this particular woman and in being freely received by her, gives to himself the identity of her *husband* and to her the identity of his *wife*, whereby the woman, in freely receiving this particular man and in giving herself unconditionally to him, gives to herself the identity of his *wife* and to him the identity of her *husband*, and whereby both the man and woman give to themselves irrevocably the identity of *spouses*. In and through the free,

---

[1] Pope John Paul II, "Nuptial Meaning of the Body", General Audience of January 9, 1980, in *Original Unity of Man and Woman: Catechesis on Genesis* (Boston: St. Paul Editions, 1981), p. 103. In this address the Holy Father is explicitly speaking about the Yahwist narrative of creation in Genesis 2, but his words also apply to the Priestly narrative in Genesis 1.

self-determining choice to marry, the man and the woman establish each other in their uniqueness. They make each other *to be irreplaceable and nonsubstitutable spouses.*

As John Paul II notes in his *Letter*, free choice is at the heart of marital consent, a choice made possible only because man—male and female—has the identity of a person with *"the capacity to live in truth and in love"* (no. 8). That free choice is at the heart of marital consent is clearly brought out, he observes, in the second chapter of Genesis (see no. 8). In another of his writings, the Holy Father has commented at more length on this crucially important point. In Genesis 2 we read that the first man, on awakening from the deep sleep into which the Lord God had put him when he fashioned the first woman from his ribs, exclaimed: "This at last is bone of my bones and flesh of my flesh. . . . For this reason a man shall leave father and mother and cleave to his wife, and the two shall become one flesh" (Gen 2:23–24; cf. *Man and Woman*, no. 10). Commenting on this passage, John Paul II observed: "The formulation of Genesis 2:24 indicates not only that human beings, created as man and woman, have been created for unity, but also that precisely this *unity, through which they become 'one flesh,' has from the beginning the character of a union that derives from a choice.* We read, in fact, 'A man will leave his father and his mother and unite to his wife.' While the man, by virtue of generation, belongs 'by nature' to his father and mother, 'he unites,' by contrast, with his wife (or she with her husband) by choice" (10.2, p. 168).

Precisely because marriage comes into existence through the irrevocable gift of the man and the woman to each other as irreplaceable and nonsubstitutable spouses, we can understand that the *indissolubility* of marriage is ontologically grounded. It is rooted in the very *being* of the man and the woman, in their freely chosen *identity* as husbands and wives, as persons made irreplaceable and nonsubstitutable in each other's life. Once a man and a woman have given their irrevocable, personal consent to marriage and established each other as absolutely irreplaceable and nonsubstitutable in their lives, they have done something that they cannot undo: they cannot divest themselves of their identity as husbands and wives, as spouses. They simply cannot *unspouse* themselves.

They have made the "sincere gift of self" to one another. "The indissolubility of marriage flows ... from the very essence of that gift" (*Letter*, no. 11). They cannot make themselves to be ex-husbands and ex-wives any more than I can make myself to be an ex-father to the children whom I have begotten. I may be a bad father, a terrible father, but I am still the father of my children. I may be a bad husband, a terrible husband, but I am still my wife's *husband*, because I have irrevocably given this identity myself. I have made her irreplaceable and nonsubstitutable in my life, and she has made me irreplaceable and nonsubstitutable in hers. We have done so because we have freely chosen *to be* married, *to be* husband and wife; we have freely chosen to unite our lives, for better, for worse, in sickness and in health, until *death* do us part. Marriage is, thus, a *person-affirming reality*. It is, as John Paul II reminds us, a "covenant of persons in love" (no. 7), and its *"indissoluble character ...* [is] the *basis of the common good of the family"* (no. 7).

2. Marriage: A Love-enabling Reality

Marriage comes into existence *through* an act of love, through the sincere *"gift of one person to another person....* Without this [sincere gift of one person to another person], marriage would be empty; whereas a communion of persons [is] built upon this logic" (no. 11), the pope said in one of his audiences. A few weeks earlier he noted that in marriage "man and woman are so firmly united as to become ... 'one flesh' (Gen 2:24). Male and female in their physical constitution, the two human subjects, even though physically different, *share equally in the capacity to live 'in truth and in love'* ... and thus express the maturity proper to persons created in the image and likeness of God" (*Letter*, no. 8).

And marriage enables husband and wife to give one another the love unique and exclusive to spouses, namely, conjugal love, which is human, total, faithful and exclusive until death, and fertile.[2] Indeed, the deepening of conjugal love is an integral aspect

---

[2] On this see *Gaudium et spes*, nos. 49–50, and *Humanae vitae*, no. 9.

of the common good of marriage and the family. "The words of [marital] consent", John Paul II affirms, "define the common good of the *couple and of the family*. First, the common good of the spouses: love, fidelity, honor, the permanence of their union until death—'all the days of my life'" (no. 10).

The depths of conjugal love, made possible by marriage, are revealed by Jesus himself. Jesus identified himself as the "Bridegroom" (cf. Mt 9:15). By doing so, the Holy Father points out, "Jesus reveals the essence of God and confirms his immense love for mankind. But the choice of this image also throws light indirectly on the profound truth of spousal love. Indeed, by using this image in order to speak about God, Jesus shows to what extent the fatherhood and the love of God are reflected in the love of man and a woman united in marriage" (no. 18). He began his public ministry at Cana in Galilee, taking part in a wedding banquet. By doing so "[h]e thus wishes to make clear *to what extent the truth about the family is part of God's Revelation and the history of salvation. . . .* At Cana in Galilee Jesus is, as it were, the *herald of the divine truth about marriage*, that truth on which the human family can rely, gaining reassurance amid all the trials of life" (no. 18).

Moreover, he "proclaims the truth about marriage again when, speaking to the Pharisees, he explains how the love which comes from God, a tender and spousal love, *gives rise to profound and radical demands*" (no. 18).

Spousal love, beautiful and tender, is a *demanding* love, requiring husbands and wives to be utterly faithful to one another and to grow ever more deeply in their exclusive love for one another, which is an integral part of the common good of marriage and the family. Spousal love is, in fact, the *life-giving principle* or form of marriage. It is essential to the establishment of marriage inasmuch as the act bringing marriage into being is an act of self-giving love, the "sincere gift of one person to another person". And within the conjugal community—the *communio personarum* (cf. no. 7)—established by this act of marital consent, spousal love abides as its life-giving principle, owed by virtue of the very consent that has generated it. Moreover, the absence of conjugal love within a marriage, while tragic, does not destroy this love, for it remains *in principle* as an *intrinsic requirement* of the marriage. As Vatican Council II put the matter: "the intimate union [of the spouses], as the mutual gift of persons, as well as the good of the children . . . *require* the full fidelity of the spouses and *demand* their indissoluble unity."[3] This love, "ratified by mutual faith", must be "indissolubly faithful amidst the prosperities and adversities of both body and spirit".[4]

Moreover, and this is of paramount significance, husbands and wives, who are *required* to give to one another spousal love, *are capable of doing so because they are married.* Marriage, in other words, *enables* them to give this kind of love to one another.[5] Husbands and wives can fulfill themselves, become fully the beings God wills them to be, only if they shape their married lives in accordance with the truth: and the truth is that they have become "one flesh" through their own free and self-determining choice. They have given to each other the "sincere gift of self". Their marital union is an earthly image of the *communio personarum* that is the Triune God. With the never-failing help of Christ, who is, as St. Thomas reminds us, "our best and wisest friend",[6] they can be true to their marital commitment. "[T]he Bridegroom is with them", as our Holy Father emphasizes in his loving *Letter to Families* (no. 18).

Indeed, precisely because marriage is a *love-enabling* reality "[t]he 'civilization of love' . . . bound up with the family" is not, the Holy Father emphasizes, a "utopia". It is not a utopia because love "is entrusted to man and woman, in the sacrament of matrimony, as the basic principle of their 'duty', and it becomes the foundation of their mutual responsibility: first as spouses, then as father and mother. . . . *Through the family passes the primary current*

---

[3] *Gaudium et spes*, no. 48, par. 1.

[4] Ibid., no. 49, par. 2.

[5] On spousal love as the life-giving principle of marriage and on marriage as a reality that enables a man and a woman to give each other this kind of love see Garcia de Haro, *Marriage and Family*, 234–56. See also Gil Hellín, "El lugar propio del amor," 1–35.

[6] Thomas Aquinas, *Summa theologiae*, I–II, q. 108, a. 4, sed contra: "Christus est maxime sapiens et amicus."

of the civilization of love, which finds therein its 'social foundations'" (no. 15).

3. Marriage: A Life-giving Reality

The Triune God is the Lord and Giver of life. And the human family, rooted in the marriage of one man and one woman, "has its origin", John Paul II declares, "in the same love with which the Creator embraces the created world.... [In fact], [t]he *only-begotten Son*, of one substance with the Father, '*God from God*, and Light from Light', *entered into human history through the family*" (*Letter*, no. 2).

Marriage is a *communio personarum* and "has to do with the personal relationship between the 'I' and the 'thou'", with their intimate union of conjugal love (no. 7). Community, as distinct from communion, "transcends this framework and moves towards a 'society,' a 'we.' The family, as a community of persons, is thus the first human 'society.' It arises whenever there comes into being the conjugal covenant of marriage, which opens the spouses to a lasting communion of love and of life, and it is brought to completion in a full and specific way with the procreation of children: the 'communion' of the spouses gives rise to the 'community' of the family" (no. 7).

Spousal love, as we have seen, is the life-giving principle of marriage. Now any love between two persons is impossible unless there is some common good that binds them together, and man's capacity for love depends on his willingness to seek a good together with others and to subordinate himself to that good for the sake of others or to others for the sake of that good.

This principle is true of every form of human love and is central to the "civilization of love". In marriage this principle is revealed in a special and unique way. For in marriage, and in marriage alone, two people, a man and a woman, are united in such a way that they become "one flesh" (Gen 2:24), i.e., the common subject, as it were, of a sexual life. To ensure that one of them does not become for the other nothing more than an object of use, a means to the attainment of some selfish end, they must share the same end or common good. We have seen already that, as the Holy Father rightly insists, the deepening of conjugal love throughout their married lives is an integral component of the common good to which husband and wife commit themselves in getting married (cf. *Letter*, no. 10).

But the procreation and education of children is also an integral component of the common good to which spouses are commited. Conjugal love is a fertile, life-giving love. When husband and wife "transmit *life to a child, a new human 'thou' becomes a part of the horizon of the 'we' of the spouses...*" (no. 11). In fact, the pope rightly observes, "*in the newborn child is realized the common good of the family....* The child becomes a gift to its brothers, sisters, parents, and entire family. *Its life becomes a gift for the very people who were givers of life* and who cannot help feel its presence, its sharing in their life and its contribution to their common good and to that of the community and the family" (no. 11). Children are indeed, as the Fathers of Vatican Council II said, "the supreme gift of marriage".[7]

It is through the "one flesh" union of husband and wife that God wills new human life to come into existence. A child, of course, can be generated through the promiscuous copulation of fornicators and adulterers, and today new human life can be "made" or "produced" in the laboratory. And a child, no matter how it is generated, is a new human person, a being of surpassing dignity and value, made in the image and likeness of God and summoned to life everlasting in union with him. But it is *not* good for new life to come into existence through acts of fornication or adultery or through new "reproductive" technologies. Fornicators and adulterers have not capacitated themselves to "welcome human life lovingly, nourish it humanely, and educate it in the love and service of God and neighbor".[8] But husbands and wives, who have freely chosen to give themselves irrevocably to one another in marriage, have capacitated themselves to do this, and

---

[7] *Gaudium et spes*, no. 50.

[8] Cf. St. Augustine, *De genesi ad literam*, 9.7 (PL 34:397).

God summons them to collaborate with him in giving life to new human persons.

The Holy Father brings out this point eloquently in a section of his *Letter* concerned with "the genealogy of the person", in which he beautifully describes the sublime mission of giving life to new human persons that God has entrusted to married men and women, husbands and wives, who are called to be fathers and mothers. He writes as follows:

> Bound up with the family is the genealogy of every individual: *the genealogy of the person.* Human fatherhood and motherhood are rooted in biology, yet at the same time transcend it.... Every act of begetting finds its primordial model in the fatherhood of God.... When a new person is born of the conjugal union of the two, he brings with him into the world a particular image and likeness of God himself: *the genealogy of the person is inscribed in the very biology of generation....* *God himself is present in human fatherhood and motherhood* quite differently than he is present in all other instances of begetting "on earth." Indeed, God alone is the source of that image and likeness".... Begetting is the continuation of creation.

> And so, both in the conception and birth of a new child, parents find themselves face to face with a "great mystery" (cf. Eph 5:32). Like his parents, the *new human being is also called* to live as a person; he is called *to a life "in truth and in love"....*

> From the very moment of conception, and then of birth, the new human being is meant *to express fully his humanity,* to "find himself" as a person. [And God wills] *to lavish upon man a sharing in his own divine life....* By his very genealogy, the person created in the image and likeness of God *exists "for his own sake",* and reaches fulfillment precisely by *sharing in God's life....* [Parents must therefore] *want the new human creature in the same way as the Creator wants him:* "for himself" (no. 9).

Marriage, precisely because it is a communion of persons united by spousal love, is by its very nature ordered to the procreation and education of children. It enables husbands and wives not only to welcome new life lovingly but also to nourish it humanely and to educate it in the love and service of God and neighbor, to give it a home where it can take root and grow in the "civilization of love".

Spousal love is intrinsically life-giving, and the intimate union of husband and wife in the marital act is indissolubly both unitive and procreative. Consequently, when they freely choose to engage in this act, "husband and wife are called to confirm in a responsible way *the mutual gift* of self which they have made to each other in the marriage covenant. The logic of the *total gift of self to the other* involves a potential openness to procreation.... *The intimate truth of this gift* must always be *safeguarded*" (no. 12).

In other words, when a married couple freely chooses to engage in the marital act, an act expressing and confirming their one-flesh union, they must be open to the "goods" and "blessings" of marriage, namely, faithful spousal love and the good of children. Were they deliberately to do something, either in anticipation of their conjugal union, during it, or in the development of its consequences, precisely to impede procreation,[9] their union would not truly be marital; it would not be an unconditional, unreserved gift of self. It is an anti-love kind of act.[10] In addition, it is an anti-life kind of act inasmuch as its precise point is to impede the beginning of a new human life; should new life be given despite the effort to impede it, it would come into the world as "unwanted". It would not be "lovingly received" as it ought to be.[11]

In educating the new life that God has given to them, parents are God's very own co-workers. Indeed, "*through Christ* all

[9] This is precisely the way Pope Paul VI defines contraception in *Humanae vitae*, no. 14, namely, as "every action, which either in anticipation of the conjugal act, or in its accomplishment, or in the development of its natural consequences, proposes [*intendat* is the Latin term used], either as end or as means, to impede procreation [*ut procreatio impediatur* is the Latin text]".

[10] Pope John Paul II has frequently developed this idea, namely that contraception by a married couple violates conjugal love and makes the marital act a "lie" insofar as it simulates and does not truly express the sincere gift of self. An excellent summary of his thought on this subject is provided by Smith, *Humanae Vitae: A Generation Later*, 230–65.

[11] For a development of this theme see Grisez et al., "Every Marital Act", 365–426.

education ... *becomes part of God's own saving pedagogy*, which ... culminates in the Paschal Mystery of the Lord's death and resurrection" (no. 16). Children are to "honor" their parents. "Honor is essentially", John Paul II says, "an attitude to unselfishness ... a 'sincere gift of person to person'". And not only should children honor the parents who have, through God's will, given them life, their mothers and fathers "should act in such a way that [their] life *will merit the honor* of [their] children" (no. 15).

Marriage, which has its source in God, the Lord and Giver of life, is indeed a *life-giving* reality.

4. Marriage: A Sanctifying Reality

The Holy Father, as already noted, emphasizes that Jesus, by identifying himself as a "Bridegroom", not only "reveals the essence of God and confirms his immense love for mankind" but also "throws light ... on the profound truth of spousal love". By participating in the wedding feast at Cana he wished, as John Paul II notes, "to make clear *to what extent the truth about the family is part of God's revelation and the history of salvation*" (*Letter*, no. 18). The author of the Epistle to the Ephesians considers marriage a great mystery (Eph 5:32) "because it expresses *the spousal love of Christ for his Church*" (no. 19). Husbands are to love their wives as Christ loved the Church "and gave himself up for her, that he might sanctify her, having cleansed her by the washing of water with the word" (Eph 5:25–26).

Commenting on this passage, John Paul II says that here the Apostle Paul is talking about baptism, "which he discusses at length in the Letter to the Romans, where he presents it as a sharing in the death of Christ leading to a sharing in his life (cf. Rom 6:3–4). In this sacrament [baptism] the believer *is born* as a new man, for baptism has the power to communicate new life, the very life of God" (no. 19). Christian husbands and wives thus find in Christ, the pope says, "*the point of reference for their spousal love....* The 'great mystery,' which is the Church and humanity in Christ, does not exist apart from the 'great mystery' expressed in the 'one flesh' (cf. Gen 2:24; Eph 5:31–32), that is, in the reality of marriage and the family" (no. 19).

Thus it is that the family based on the sacramental marriage of Christian husbands and wives is in truth a "domestic church" (no. 19). It has been commissioned by Christ himself, as John Paul II had earlier explained at length in his apostolic exhortation *Familiaris consortio*, to participate in a unique and indispensable way in the saving mission of the universal Church. It is to do this by sharing profoundly in Christ's threefold mission as prophet, priest, and king and by being a believing and evangelizing community, a community in dialogue with God, and a community serving others by transforming the world through the redemptive love of Christ.[12]

Precisely because marriage is a *sanctifying* reality, the family built on it intimately shares in the "history of 'fairest love'", a history that began, in a certain way, with the first human couple and culminated paradigmatically in the marital union of Mary and Joseph, thanks to whom "the *mystery of the Incarnation* and, together with it, the mystery of the Holy Family, *come to be profoundly inscribed in the spousal love of husband and wife*" (no. 20; italics in original). Marriage is indeed a *sanctifying* reality.

The Family and Society

The family is the "basic cell" of society (no. 4). It is the "first and basic expression of man's *social nature*" (no. 7). The family indeed, "more than any other human reality" [is] "the place where an individual can exist 'for himself' through the sincere gift of self. This is why it remains a social institution which neither can nor should be replaced: it is the 'sanctuary of life'" (no. 11; cf. *Centessimus annus*, 39). It is "*the center and the heart of the*

[12] On this see *Familiaris consortio*, nos. 49–64. For a commentary, see Patricia A. May and William E. May, "The Family as a Saved and Saving Community: A Specific and Original Ecclesial Role", in *The Christian Family in the World Today: Proceedings of the Sixteenth Convention of the Fellowship of Catholic Scholars* (Steubenville, Ohio: Franciscan University of Steubenville Press, 1994), pp. 179–201.

civilization of love" (no. 13). Because it is all this, the family renders the larger human society an absolutely indispensable and priceless service.

The family built upon the marriage of one man and one woman thus expects from society "*a recognition of its identity* and an acceptance of its *status as a subject in society*" (no. 17). It has its own sovereignty, albeit conditioned, and it must be respected for what it is. It is the bearer of rights within society that must be honored. While the rights of the family are intimately linked to the inviolable rights of persons, they are, John Paul II insists, "*not simply the sum total* of the rights of the person, since the family is *much more* than the sum of individual members. It is a community of parents and children, and at times a community of several generations. For this reason its 'status as a subject,' which is grounded in God's plan, gives rise to and calls for certain proper and specific rights" (no. 17).

Here I cannot go into detail with respect to the rights of the family that must be respected by the international community, the nation, and the state: rights such as those of the parents to procreate and to educate their own children, to a living wage, etc. Yet it is important, in coming to a close of this overview of Pope John Paul II's *Letter to Families*, to focus on two issues. The first of these concerns the rights of women and mothers. The Holy Father is particularly eloquent about these rights. He stresses the importance of acknowledging and appreciating the "*work women do within the family unit*". He writes:

> The "toil" of a woman who, having given birth to a child, nourishes and cares for that child and devotes herself to its upbringing, particularly in the early years, is so great as to be comparable to any professional work. This ought to be clearly stated and upheld, no less than any other labor right. Motherhood, because of all the hard work it entails, should be recognized as giving the right to financial benefits at least equal to those of other kinds of work undertaken in order to support the family during such a delicate phase of its life (no. 17).

The second issue concerns the dangers facing marriage and society itself from "permissiveness" regarding the identity of "marriage" and "family". John Paul II is emphatic and correct in declaring that the marriage of one man and one woman who have freely given themselves irrevocably to one another is the rock on which the family is built, and that only a union of this kind can be recognized and ratified as marriage in society. But today there is, on part of some powerful elite, an attempt to confer the dignity of marriage—along with the rights pertaining to it—to unions of "free love", i.e., unions that endure only so long as they are pleasing to their partners, and even to homosexual liaisons. Referring to this growing tendency, John Paul II vigorously declares that "[n]o human society can run the risk of permissiveness in fundamental issues regarding the nature of marriage and the family! Such moral permissiveness cannot fail to damage the authentic requirements of peace and communion among people" (*Letter*, no. 17).

In his *Letter* the Holy Father identifies several basic dangers to family life today: a rampant individualism utterly opposed to true personalism (cf. no. 14); the ethic of utilitarianism that treats persons as an object of use (cf. no. 14), a dualism reminiscent of the ancient ideologies of gnosticism and Manichaeanism (cf. no. 19). All these evils encourage selfishness and hedonism, give rise to the plague of divorce and the anti-life mentality so manifest in the widespread practice of contraception and abortion. In many ways human society today, the Holy Father points out, is "sick" because it has lost sight of the truth about man, the truth "about what man and woman really are as persons" (no. 20). The "civilization of love" is threatened by a "civilization of death". But we are to have hope, because the *Bridegroom is with us*. If we abide in God's love, honor marriage and the family built on it, we can develop the "civilization of love", a civilization in which all human persons, born or unborn, of whatever condition or race or sex, will indeed be wanted and loved as a person made in the image and likeness of God and called to life eternal as a member of God's own family.

INDEX

abortion: and contraceptive revolution, xiv–xv, 15–16; and fifth moral criterion for families, 15–16; Paul VI prophetic warnings, xiv, 70–71

Address to the Italian Union of Midwives (1951) (Pius XII), 25

Adler, Mortimer, 2n2

adultery: and concupiscence, 123–25; between married persons "in the heart", 123–25; Paul VI on contraception and marital infidelity, 70; and Sermon on the Mount, 123, 125

Akerlof, George, xiv–xvi

Allen, Prudence, 43

American Civil Liberties Union (ACLU), 69

amor, 146–49

Ashley, Benedict, 47, 49, 88–89

Atkinson, Joseph, 91, 93

Augustine, St., 2n3, 6on9, 64, 83n15, 124

baptism, 95, 163–64

Benedict XVI's teaching on marriage and family life, xix, 135–50; on bodily nature of humans, 137–38, 149; on conjugal love and joining of body and soul, 149; on development of conciliar teachings on marriage, 144; on the ecclesial community's responsibilities toward the family, 143; encyclical *Deus caritas est*, 141, 142, 145, 146–49; on the family as foundation of society, 143; on Genesis accounts of creation, 148; on God's union with humankind and the sacramentality of marriage, 138; on the human embryo as person, 142; on the indissolubility of marriage, 145; and John Paul II's *Familiaris consortio*, 137–38, 139, 141; and John Paul II's Theology of the Body, 136, 143, 145, 149; on juridical dimension of marriage, 144–46; on the love uniting *eros* and *agape*, 142, 145, 146–49; papal addresses, 135–46;